finding MOMMY *bliss*

Discovering unexpected joy in everyday moments.

GENNY HEIKKA

Hallway Publishing
2701 Del Paso Road, 130-92
Sacramento, CA 95835

hallwaypublishing.com
Contact Information: info@thehallwayproject.com

Finding Mommy Bliss

COPYRIGHT © 2014 by Genny Heikka

First Edition, May 2014

Cover Art by Ben De Rienzo
Typeset by Odyssey Books

Paperback ISBN: 978-1-941058-04-6
Hardback ISBN: 978-1-941058-05-3

Published in the United States of America

CONTENTS

To Katie and Luke
You have changed my life in more ways
than words or chapters will ever describe
Being your mom is bliss

To Mike
My soul mate and constant support
I never would have been able to reach for my dreams
without your encouragement along the way
You are an amazing man, an incredible dad,
and I love you

finding
MOMMY
bliss

Discovering unexpected joy
in everyday moments.

INTRODUCTION

There is bliss in being a mom.
Sometimes, we just need a little help finding it.

I'm sitting here as I write this, thinking of you on the other end of these pages. You, the mom who may be grabbing a few minutes to read while your kids are napping, or at school, or simply in the other room playing.

You, the mom who might be longing for a minute (or even a few seconds) of peace and quiet.

You, the mom who might be worn out, stretched thin, tired, searching for more purpose, more happiness, more . . . *something*.

Being a mom can make you feel like that, I know. After all, it's a vulnerable place to be: sacrificing everything, putting your life (and yourself) on hold for a while, and opening your heart to a love more powerful than you could ever imagine.

Wherever you are today, mom—weary, exhausted, frustrated, hopeful, searching—I'm glad you're starting this journey. And you know what? You might be surprised as you move forward (and it might be hard to imagine right now), but with each page you turn and each step you take to intentionally find more joy in motherhood, that peace you're longing for will come.

And the bliss will come, too.

Because being a happy mom isn't about sailing through motherhood. It's not about having it all together or having the best kids. And it's definitely not about perfection. Experiencing mommy-bliss—the deep joy that motherhood can so freely give—is so much about perspective and choices. It's about loving the mom that you are (because you are the exact mom your kids need). It's about learning to laugh at things you might not find funny at first (because parenting is full of those things). It's about letting yourself cry when you need to (because you're worth it). And it's about learning to love the best that you can, every day.

Being a mom is a blessed calling and God has amazing joy for us in the journey, even in the middle of the messy and mundane. And just like the journey of motherhood isn't meant to be walked alone, this book isn't meant to be read alone. It's meant to be shared, like those stories we tell each other at play dates or over coffee.

It's often those stories that encourage and inspire me the most. And I hope this book will encourage you in that way too. I hope it will inspire you to come alongside other moms and share your own stories, whether they're funny or sad or embarrassing or painful. And I hope it will help you discover the joy in your everyday moments. Because bliss sometimes hides in the corners of motherhood—in the feel of your baby's sleepy head on your shoulder as you carry her through the grocery store pushing the cart with one hand, in the quiet singing of your preschooler as he sits in the corner during his timeout, or in the smile of your eighteen-year-old as he walks across the stage to get his high school diploma that, after all the challenges he had in school, you weren't sure he was going to get. Because *those* kinds of moments—even though they're sometimes sandwiched in between a whole lot of stress—*are* bliss.

We're in this together, mom. The experience of motherhood is unique to each one of us, but the love we have for our kids is universal. And once you have kids and they start to grow up, you suddenly learn the truth behind the saying "time flies." Well, except on those days where you're counting the minutes until everyone goes to bed so you can get *one single second of peace and quiet!* Except on *those* days, time *does* fly. One minute you have a baby and the next thing you know, she's a teenager. And even though I'm no expert, I *do* know it goes that fast.

I also know that I'm a whole lot better at mommy-hood with others by my side.

Others like you.

So let's set out on this journey and look for the moments of joy together.

Because there *is* bliss in being a mom.

Sometimes, we just need a little help finding it . . .

Tip #1

Identify Where You Are
(or: Who knew being a mom would be like this?!)

"Being a mother means that your heart
is no longer yours;
it wanders wherever your children go."
—Author Unknown

Bliss
1. perfect happiness; great joy
2. paradise, heaven

Bliss?

Are you kidding?

There's paradise and heaven to be found in the middle of diapers, temper tantrums, arguing kids, and piles of laundry?

I know that's what you might be thinking right now. And the whole idea of mommy-bliss might seem a little far-fetched.

But, actually, it's not.

And, no, I'm not kidding.

The problem is, sometimes we miss it.

It's as simple as that; we miss the bliss. We get caught up in rushing around from soccer to swim team, from the grocery store to the doctor's office, from one load of laundry or dishes to the next, and we don't have time to think about what's so magical about motherhood. We're just trying to get everyone fed, everyone to sleep, or everyone to clean their rooms—for once in their lives.

If that's you, don't be hard on yourself. I've been there plenty of times. Because life is busy and motherhood is busier. The schedule never seems to slow down and the to-do list never seems to get done. And any sort of bliss might seem totally out of reach. Whether you have one child or eight, whether you work outside of the house or stay at home, whether you have babies or teens, whether you're raising your own kids or someone else's, whether you've adopted or not, home-schooled or not, are single or married, have "little angels" or "wild things" running around your house, being a mom can be one of the most rewarding experiences of your life.

But it can also be one of the most challenging.

And the most overwhelming.

And the most humbling.

Who knew we could learn so much from these little human beings? Like how to function on only a few hours of sleep? And how to help with homework, make dinner, answer the phone, and look for the missing binky—all at the same time?

Who knew that being a mom came with its own set of priorities and sacrifices, or that it would teach us so much about compromising and negotiating? And about the fact that, most of the time, we *shouldn't* be compromising and negotiating because we're the moms, right?

Who knew that being a parent would be such a balancing act? We want to be organized, but we feel like we're not. We want to be productive, but we never seem to be able to get it all done. We want to be consistent, but sometimes we're exhausted. We want to make the right decisions, but sometimes we don't know what the right decisions are. We want to be role models, but we're far from perfect. We want time to ourselves, but our kids need our time.

Most of all, we want to be good moms. And we just don't know if we are. We get frustrated and lose our patience and spend some days looking forward to the *next* phase of parenting, when our kids will finally be out of diapers, or when they'll finally be out of strollers, or when they'll finally be driving themselves around. When things will be easier and we will be happier and we can get back to feeling like ourselves.

We hope.

Parenting is like that though. It's amazing, fulfilling, rewarding . . . exhausting and challenging. One minute you're watching your daughter run off to school in her knee-high socks with her ponytail swinging and a big smile on her face, and you're choking back tears at how cute she is. And just a few hours later, you're ready to pull your hair out (and hers) because she's arguing with you for the tenth time that day.

We love our kids—we *do* . . . more than we can put into words. But we're human. And in spite of our love, we get impatient, stressed, worried, or just plain tired. When things get tough, it can be hard to show our love, and—let's admit—during those *really* tough times, even feel it. But it's then that finding the bliss in motherhood is really about choices—deliberate choices that determine what kind of attitude we have and what kind of impact we make on our families.

I know right now you may be stuck in the weeds of motherhood, surrounded by crying toddlers, piles of sippy cups, arguing kids, and a house full of chaos. But raise your eyes for a minute, mom. Look past the mess, past the crying, past the busyness, and fast-forward five, ten, maybe even twenty years. Sooner than you know, your kids will be grown. They will be on their own out in the world, living the lives they were made to live. And you—their mom—will have helped prepare them for that. Even though it might not feel like it right now, you are shaping their souls and building their character. You are raising leaders, teachers, influencers, artists, writers, managers, moms, dads—whatever they grow up to be—to go out and make a difference in the world. So I encourage you, even though it's hard sometimes, at this starting point of your journey to finding more joy as a mom, keep your eyes focused on the big picture and the goal ahead, and—I promise you—bliss will sneak up on you in the most amazing ways.

"Whenever I held my newborn baby in my arms, I used to think that what I said and did to him could have an influence not only on him, but on all whom he met, not only for a day or a month or a year, but for all eternity— a very challenging and exciting thought for a mother."
—Rose Kennedy

Be More Blissful: Parenting doesn't always feel blissful, but there is joy to be found, if only you look. Your role as a mom is important. You are not invisible; you are highly valued. As you head out on this journey, stop for a minute, remind yourself how important your role is, and make a commitment to look for the bliss in being a mom. Then be ready for the new joy you are about to discover!

You have a special calling as a mom. Even if you feel invisible and unappreciated sometimes, everything you do matters, not only to your kids, but to the world. So how do you keep the stresses and worries of motherhood from swallowing your joy and banishing your bliss? First, you need to understand where you are today.

In the same way you need to have a starting point when you're getting directions to somewhere, you need to know where you're at as a mom so you can identify what areas you might need to grow in, and what you might need to focus on.

Below is a questionnaire that can help. Take a few minutes and fill it out. I encourage you to be honest (you don't have to show it to anyone if you don't want to!). It is simply a tool for *you* that will be a point of reference as you read further. So go find a quiet corner, grab a cup of coffee or tea, and spend some time answering the questions . . .

WHERE AM I NOW?

Most of the time, I feel _____
about being a mom.

If I had to pick one word that describes my daily
attitude, it would be:_____.

When it comes to parenting, I wish I was better at:
_____.

When it comes to parenting, I know I am good at:
_____.

I love_____with my kids.

I don't like_____with my kids.

I want to give my kids more_____.

I know I should give my kids less_____.

If I could _____
I would be more fulfilled and happy.

My greatest fear as a mom is_____.

The environment in my home is usually

_____.

Something that holds me back from being happy is
_____.

My kids would describe me as_____.

My bliss-rate as a mom is:
Miserable .... Blissful
1   2   3   4   5   6   7   8   9   10

To think about:
– Am I happy with my parenting or do I feel over-whelmed and as though I'm not doing a good job?
– Am I satisfied with my overall attitude and perspective toward motherhood or are there changes I need to make?

Reflections: _____
_____
_____
_____

Mom-to-Mom: Maybe some light bulbs went off for you as a result of filling out those blanks. Maybe you realized just how stressed or frustrated you are as a mom. Or maybe you realized you're happier than you thought. Did you have any personal revelations? What were they? If you're reading this book with a group of other moms, and if you want to share your answers, take a few minutes to discuss. I promise you; whatever you're feeling, you're not alone!

Heart-to-Heart: "Search me, God, and know my heart; test me and know my anxious thoughts."

—*Psalm 139:23 NIV*

Even if we aren't always in touch with how we are feeling, God is. He knows how you feel right now and He can handle whatever you're going through. Have you acknowledged your own feelings? Have you considered asking Him for help in your parenting or other areas of your life? He's there, waiting and ready.

A Mom's Prayer: *God, You know what I'm going through right now and how I'm feeling. Please open my heart to what You have for me as a mom. Give me the wisdom to hear Your voice above the chaos and to feel Your grace covering my parenting. I look forward to what You are doing right now in me, and in my family. I know Your timing is perfect. Help me to find more joy in my role as a parent. I want to be the kind of mom You created me to be. Amen.*

Tip #2

Love Perceptively, Here and Now
(And you'll see the re-gifts!)

"Taking joy in living is a woman's best cosmetic."
—Rosalind Russell

Maybe one of the things you just realized from doing the exercise in the last chapter is that you are pretty stressed as a mom. Maybe it's been a while since you felt like you truly took joy in living. In the middle of all the juggling we do, it can be easy for the schedule to take over.

But getting caught up in (or weighed down by) the to-do list is one of the surest ways to miss the bliss. So much of being blissful is about the way we see things, and *what* we see or miss.

My husband Mike's grandma, Nana Mae, was someone who never lost sight of the beauty around her. Her personality matched her bright red hair and there wasn't a time you were with her that she didn't compliment you or tell you how pretty something was.

I'll never forget the time Mike and I drove her to Los Angeles for Christmas when she was eighty-nine years old. We were at a gas station along I-5, which is a long highway in California, when Nana pointed out the window and said, "Beautiful!" I looked to see what she was talking about, but all I could see was a green garbage truck pulled over near the gas station. She pointed at it. "That's a *beautiful* green," she said. I smiled. She was talking about a *garbage truck*, but, still, she saw the beauty in it.

As moms, we can choose whether or not we see the beauty in what sometimes feels like the garbage in our days—the sink full of dishes, the arguing kids, the crazy running around. And we play a huge role in whether or not we set a "beautiful" tone for our families. One thing that can help us in this area is loving perceptively, here and now. And one thing that can help us do that is paying attention to how our kids see the world. When we look at things from their perspectives, we have the opportunity to notice, almost as if for the first time, the wonder around us. I call it discovering the re-gifts— those times we get little glimpses of life from our kids' perspectives as they discover the world around them, and we get to *re*discover it too.

When my daughter Katie, who is now a teenager, was about eight years old, a trail of ants showed up on the tile in the entryway of our house after a big rain. As I started wiping the ants up, she offered to do it instead. Happily, I let her. But a little while later, when I looked over to see how she was doing, I realized she wasn't wiping them up at all; she was bending over the tile floor with a magnifying glass, whispering something. My first reaction was impatience. I wanted the ants *gone* and I had visions of more of them crawling into our house while she sat there watching. So I went over to her and asked her what she was doing.

"Oh, *Mommy*," she said, looking up at me and smiling, "This ant is *so* sweet. He's carrying his friend *all* the way across the floor." Her eyes got wide. "He puts him down and takes a little rest and then picks him right back up. He's *so good*, Mommy."

I have to tell you, even though we're talking about *ants* here, her sweet little words tugged at my heart. And instead of being irritated and rushing her to clean the ants up, I ended up crouched next to her, watching them too. And—I kid you not—I got a lump in my throat. More from the glimpse into my daughter's heart than from the struggling ant, but a lump all the same.

I could've easily missed that moment—that here and now. I could've yelled at her to get cleaning. I could've told her ants aren't sweet. I could've decided to do the job myself. But, instead, I got to pause and appreciate how *she* saw the situation. And in that, there was a moment of unexpected joy.

If we miss these kinds of re-gifts, we miss the bliss.

My son Luke, who is twelve, had a project in his first-grade class years ago where he'd been asked to draw a picture and write a story about what he wants to be when he grows up. This is what he wrote:

> *I am a bisnis man. I'm wareing a tan shirt. I am on my desk. I am working. I Just got off my two day vacation. I love this job because my dad does it and he maxe milyens.*

From his perspective, Mike works on *top* of his desk and takes a lot of two-day vacations. And, even better, he makes "milyens." Ha!

We all know there will come a day when our kids will view things differently than they do now. At some point—and some of us may even remember exactly when—this happened to us. We started to play less and plan more. Our perspectives evolved and our priorities changed. And, while growing up is good and necessary in its own way, it comes with a more serious view of the world and everything in it. But when we can stop and notice—*really* notice—how precious our kids' perspectives are, it fills us with a new appreciation and wonder for the here and now.

Think about it for a minute: How differently would you feel if you started to look at your life through your kids' eyes? Or if you have teenagers, from their eyes when they were younger. Would your house seem bigger or more beautiful? Would your talents seem more amazing? Would you feel more capable, successful, *wonderful?*

To our kids, we are the *bomb*. We're the cooks, chauffeurs, house-cleaners, doctors, coaches, teachers . . . there's nothing we can't do. So why do we feel so limited sometimes? So untalented? So unremarkable? Why are we so critical of ourselves?

We see our kids as amazing, and we want them to believe that about themselves, but we forget that they see *us* as amazing. We forget that we *are* amazing. Caring for another human being for eighteen years or more is no small feat.

So remember, mom: you *are* the bomb, *here and now.*

If you struggle with seeing yourself as amazing, don't be discouraged. It's something you can learn. The more we love perceptively in the here and now and understand how our kids view things, the more we will appreciate the unique people they are . . . and the unique people *we* are too.

A few years ago, when I was out running errands, the traffic light just ahead of me turned yellow. I immediately slowed down, while the driver in the truck next to me gunned it. He sailed through the intersection and I sat stopped at the crosswalk, both before the light even turned red. And that's when I realized there are two kinds of people in this world: those who put on the breaks and those who speed up when the light is almost red. For anything that involves going fast or taking risks that might endanger my life, I fall into the breaks category.

There've been many times I've wished I wasn't like this, though. Many times I've wished I was more *daring* and *adventurous.* And I'm not talking about traffic lights. I'm talking about trying new things like skydiving or whitewater rafting or *exciting* things like that. Why don't I want to go cliff jumping or scuba diving?

And why is it when I'm wakeboarding or snow skiing (which I don't even do anymore), I worry about falling?

I'm fast-paced in my daily life, and I jump into challenges full-force, but take me to an amusement park and I'll pick the kiddy train over the rollercoaster any day. I'm obviously missing whatever gene makes people enjoy speed and danger. And I used to be hard on myself about this.

But having kids has helped. In understanding their personalities, I've also come to understand my own better. When Luke first started snow skiing, he pointed his skis straight downhill and went as fast as he could. Katie, on the other hand, preferred side-to-side S curves. Luke used to say he wanted to hang glide and drive a race car and invent a jet-powered backpack that can make people fly when he grew up. Katie had "safer" aspirations . . . to be a mommy, a doctor, an artist, an actress.

Seeing what matters individually to Katie and Luke has really helped me notice and appreciate the individuals they are. And it's helped me to appreciate who *I* am too, rather than comparing myself to others and wishing I was more this way or that. Sure, I could push myself and do something crazy like bungee jumping (see how I call it *crazy?*). And maybe someday I will. Maybe it *would* be fun. Who am I kidding? I'll never really do it. But that's okay.

> **Be More Blissful: Lighten up today. Instead of being critical of yourself or your kids, give everyone a break. Think of one thing you appreciate about yourself. Think of one thing you appreciate about each of your kids, too—something that makes them unique. Then tell them!**

I'm okay. And so are you, mom. You're *more* than okay. You're the wonderful, amazing mom that your kids think you are!

What defines your joy, mom? Is it how you feel at the moment? I have to admit, sometimes I let my feelings get the best of me, and they definitely end up impacting my mood.

I was out driving a while ago when I saw a license plate frame that said "14 kids and still going strong." My thought was . . . *wow.* Honestly, I was feeling a little mom-frazzled at the time and it was hard for me to imagine. I was instantly full of admiration for that mama. With only two kids, I wasn't feeling strong at all.

As I drove and thought about it more, I realized just how much of how we feel about parenting is about our perspective—how we look at our situation and the events of the day—and how much we let that dictate our feelings.

I thought about the night before, when Katie had gotten home from cheer practice. It was late on a school night and I was in a *let'shurryupandgetyoutobed* mode, rushing her around. She hadn't seen me all day, and she wanted to talk. As I tucked her in, she lay in bed, chatting a mile a minute. I stood there impatiently nodding, half listening. I felt like she was talking so much just to keep me in her room.

Then it struck me that I was right. She *was* trying to keep me in her room. She wanted me there because she wanted time with me. Loving perceptively means being able to see our kids' uniqueness and what's important to them, and parent in a way that honors that. Suddenly, after realizing she needed more time with me, staying in her room a little longer was a joy, not an inconvenience. I was happy to be there, not impatient to leave. It was all about my perspective.

That mom of fourteen was still going strong, and that's perspective, too. Whether you have one child or fourteen, it can be easy to feel worn out. But if your attitude and perspective is positive, you will likely feel strong and more joyful. There is always someone who has it easier than you and there is always someone who has it harder. And when you love perceptively in the here and now, how you view your situation can be greatly impacted . . . for the better.

Mom-to-Mom: What is one re-gift you've gotten as a mom? What is one thing in your life or yourself right now that you're viewing negatively that you might view more positively if you looked at it from your kids' perspectives? Is there an area in your parenting where you know you need a perspective or attitude shift?

Heart-to-Heart: "For you created my inmost being; you knit me together in my mother's womb. I praise you because I am fearfully and wonderfully made; your works are wonderful, I know that full well."

—*Psalm 139:13-14 NIV*

Have you let these words soak in, mom? Do you truly believe them? What does it mean to you to be fearfully and wonderfully made? Do you find that easy to believe for your kids, but not for yourself?

A Mom's Prayer: *God, thank you for making me who I am. Thank you for all of my qualities, even the ones I sometimes take for granted or don't appreciate. Help me to see myself—every part of me—the way You see me . . . beautiful and wonderful. Help me to see the beauty around me too. Even when I'm exhausted, worried, or stressed, remind me of the gifts You have given me. Help me to face the challenges of being a mom with a new perspective and love in the here and now. Thank you for the gift of my children. Amen.*

Tip #3

Don't Rush the Journey
(or: Just sit tight, hold on, and enjoy the ride!)

"It's the little details that are vital. Little things make big things happen."—John Wooden

One day, our kids will move out and we'll have all the quiet we want. There will be no screaming in the back seat, no nights with everyone calling us to their rooms, no arguing teenagers, no driving everyone around . . . and I bet it will be much quieter than we want it to be. At a time when there is so much joy to be found, it's ironic that so many of us (myself included) live some days looking forward to the *next* phase of parenting, when we think things will be easier.

I remember when Katie was a toddler, Luke was a baby, and Mike was travelling a lot. I remember sometimes being overwhelmed with the constant feedings, diaper changes, nursing and crying—and just looking forward to when my kids would be older.

Yet, not too long ago, I caught myself saying to Mike as we struggled with a decision whether or not to let Katie go to a certain friend's house, "It was easier when they were little."

The grass is always greener on the other side, isn't it? There's a poem called "Present Tense" that was written by a fourteen-year-old named Jason Lehman that illustrates this so perfectly. It starts out:

It was spring, but it was summer I wanted,
The warm days and the great outdoors.
It was summer, but it was fall I wanted,
The colorful leaves, and the cool, dry air.

The poem continues like that through seasons and phases of life until, at the end, it says:

My life was over, and I never got what I wanted.

Such wisdom for a fourteen-year-old, right? (I encourage you to look it up and read the full poem; I'm sure it will get you like it got me!)

> **Be More Blissful:** I know on those crazy days when the baby won't stop crying and your two-year-old won't take a nap, it can be easy to wish for time to pass by more quickly. But slowing down and becoming more aware of how fast time is already flying can help, even on the hard days. So take a minute and pause today, mom. Soak in the moments, maybe even capturing them by writing about them in a journal or by writing a note to your kids. Take pictures of what you're doing with your family today, even if it's just an ordinary day. Because, often, the ordinary moments are the ones we end up remembering and treasuring the most.

But that's how it is for us sometimes, isn't it? So often as moms, we long for something other than what we have. We forget to pay attention to the moment right in front of us. We spend our time looking toward the future—planning, unintentionally rushing the journey, awaiting the *next* phase of parenting—and we miss the bliss along the way. But when we set out to enjoy the journey and slow down long enough to open a sliver of time in our days for mommy-bliss to find its way through . . . it will.

I saw this so clearly one night when Katie was about to go into middle school. Mike was out at a dinner meeting for work and Luke had just fallen asleep. I was tucking Katie into bed, thinking about all the things I had to get done before the next day—we'd been at her play practice that night and had gotten home later than usual. When I kissed her on the forehead and turned to leave her room, she said, "Mommy, will you stay in my room for a while?"

"Not tonight," I said instantly, not even hesitating. "It's late. And you need to get to sleep." I gave her another kiss on the forehead.

She reached her arms around my neck and hugged me. "*Please?*"

I wavered, thinking about the dishes, the laundry, and the e-mails I needed to catch up on.

"*Please?*" she asked again.

"All right," I said, sighing and giving in, "but just for a minute."

I sat down on her bed.

She reached out and held my hand. We didn't talk much. She was tired and so was I. Instead, we listened to the hum of her ceiling fan and the bubbling of her fish tank.

"Goodnight, Mommy," she said, yawning.

"Goodnight."

As I sat there, it hit me how fast she was growing up. And I realized she might not be asking me to stay in her room with her at night much longer. I wished I hadn't told her *no* so quickly. And I savored the moment, realizing that someday—someday probably too soon—these times together would be memories, and not something she asks me to do regularly.

One minute turned into two.

Then two turned into three.

I didn't want to leave.

I watched her eyes close and listened to the sound of her breathing as she fell asleep. And I was more thankful than ever for that moment . . . the moment I almost missed.

> **Be More Blissful: Don't miss the moments today, mom. Stay in your kids' rooms a little longer tonight when you tuck them in. Take that extra five minutes, or thirty, to sit with them, talk, or just be there as they fall asleep.**

I wish I could say I've never missed a special moment like that with my kids, but there have been plenty of times I have, simply because I've been rushing the journey. And most of the time, I'm not even aware of it when I'm doing it.

A while ago, when I was in the car with Luke, he asked, out of the blue, "Why did you want to be a writer, Mom?" I explained to him that writing is something I love and I told him about my dream of becoming an author. I also explained that writing is different than working at a company full-time like I used to because the flexibility gives me more time with him and Katie.

And that's when he said, "But you still work a lot, Mom. You're always on the computer."

I felt instantly convicted. In spite of the flexibility that comes with being a writer, I knew I *had* been on the computer a lot during that time. I had just broken my arm and completely torn a muscle in my leg (I'll tell you the story in chapter sixteen) and I wasn't very mobile. So I *had* been writing a lot, trying to take advantage of the downtime. But what I didn't realize was that while I was making progress focusing on my writing, I was missing moments with my kids. And Luke noticed.

When I asked him if it bothered him when I'm on the computer, he said, "It doesn't bother me that you are on the computer, Mom. I just wish you had more time to take me to the park or something."

Ouch.

I knew right then I needed to slow down and enjoy the journey with them more. I needed to be there for them, not only physically, but emotionally as well. I realized I had been getting so focused on my writing and the things I wanted to accomplish with it during my "downtime," that I hadn't been seeing the everyday moments right in front of me or the opportunities to slow down with my kids. We've all heard the saying that kids spell love T-I-M-E. It's one of the ways they feel loved. When we get too busy to spend time with them, they notice. And it impacts them.

Do I really need to be rushing Luke, reminding him to hurry up because we have a half an hour until soccer? Or telling Katie to pack her backpack for school and make sure she has her lunch in there . . . when she's already done both?

How often do I forget to slow down? How many times do I run around barking orders or reminding my kids unnecessarily to do things . . . and chase the joy right out of our house? Or miss what my kids are feeling? When Katie comes home from school and acts a little grumpy, could it be that she's had a bad day, and not that she's having a bad attitude? When Luke calls me to his room several times at bedtime, could it be because he wants to talk to me, and not because he's being difficult? When I hear, "Mom . . . ?" twenty times a day from both of them, is it because they want me to slow down, and not because they are being needy?

We need to slow down long enough to enjoy the journey . . . so we can not only see the bliss that's hiding in the everyday moments, but so we can also see (*really* see) our kids.

When Katie and Luke were younger, I took them to the gym with me one day to work out. After I was done, I went to pick them up from the play area and on my way I passed the window to the room they were in. Katie saw me through the glass, jumped up, and waved. And when I opened the door, she was standing right there at the front desk, smiling.

"Mommy!" she said, hugging me tight.

I'd only been gone for an hour, but by the way she acted, you'd guess it had been a week. This sweet greeting from her seriously melted my heart.

And it made me think . . . How do I say hello to *her*?

I thought about the morning before, when I woke her up with a quick kiss on the forehead, then launched into a very rushed, "Don't take too long getting ready because it's our day to carpool. And you need to clean your room before we leave. It looks like a tornado came through here."

I thought about when I'd picked the kids up from school that day, too. We'd walked through the park, passing others who were playing on the swings and buying ice-cream from the ice-cream truck. I shuffled Katie and Luke along, reminding them to *hurry* because we had to get to basketball. I barely registered their disappointed faces when I told them we didn't have time for ice-cream. And I realized I needed to be more aware—constantly aware—of how I greet them. Because I want to make sure when I say *hi* to my kids, or to Mike, or to *anyone* for that matter, I'm doing it in a way that really acknowledges them. I want to give the kind of greeting that focuses on that moment, not all of the things we have scheduled. And I want them to know how much I love them.

With every single *hello*.

Be More Blissful: Refuse to be hurried today. Take time to slow down, and slow your kids down too. Then notice what happens. You may just discover a new pace for your family!

Several years ago, as Katie was just finishing fifth grade, we went to Open House night at her school. I vividly remember how I stood there in her classroom, looking at all the things she made throughout the year . . . the life-sized human body, the history timelines, the intricate drawings of plant and animal cells . . . and it hit me all at once just how quickly time was passing, and how much I wanted to slow things down.

Middle school, I thought, almost not believing it. *She'll be in middle school next year.*

Another parent who hadn't seen Katie in a while came up to us. "She's gotten so *tall*," she said.

I nodded. "I know."

We passed other kids on the way out and I thought the same thing . . . they were all taller than I remembered. More mature, too. And suddenly I realized, *It's here. She's growing up. It's here.* We walked across the playground to leave the school, and I watched Katie as she ran ahead. My mind sped to the teenage years that were just around the corner. I thought about high school, and college, wanting more than anything for her to achieve her dreams, and wanting her to enjoy the journey along the way.

We left the playground and headed through the park toward our house. All around us, other families walked home too. Kids rode their bikes and played. Laughter filled the air. "Come on, Mommy," Katie called, motioning for me to hurry. I jogged to catch up, thoughts playing in my mind . . .

Even if we hit bumps in the road as she gets older, I hope I can be patient. And fair. I hope we always have a good relationship. I hope . . .

And that's when I felt something . . . her hand—not tiny like it used to be, but still small, still young—slipping into mine. I looked at her and smiled. She smiled back, unaware of the thoughts racing through my mind. We crossed the street like that, holding hands, and when we got to the other side, she pulled me toward the sidewalk and squeezed my fingers. I squeezed back and, believe me, I held on tight.

And that's what we have to do sometimes, mom. Hold on tight to the moments even as they are unfolding right in front of us, instead of letting them pass unnoticed, unappreciated, and in a hurry.

Mom-to-Mom: Do you find yourself too rushed, too stressed, and too distracted? If so, why do you think that is?

Heart-to-Heart: 'Be still and know that I am God."
—Psalm 46:10 NIV

Is it hard or easy for you to be still? When was the last time you slowed down to listen to your kids? To listen to God? What did you hear or learn?

A Mom's Prayer: *God, thank you for the reminder to be still and that You not only encourage me to slow down, You command it. Help me to pause and listen more, to You and to my kids. Help me to notice the miracles and moments around me. I don't want to miss what You have for me or my family today. Amen.*

Tip #4

Love, Even When it's Difficult
(In other words, keep calm, don't freak out,
and don't try to control everything!)

"Do I love you because you're beautiful,
or are you beautiful because I love you?"
—Richard Rodgers and Oscar Hammerstein II,
Cinderella

Some days, parenting is . . . hard.

That was my exhausted thought as I drove Katie home from swim team one night. The whole day had been a battle. I can't even remember what the issues were, but it seemed like everything had been a challenge that day. Maybe it was because we had a busy schedule and I was being impatient. Or maybe it was because she was almost eleven at the time and was becoming more independent. Whatever the reason, I was frustrated, she was mad, and it was one of those days.

So there we were, driving along, on the heels of an argument, and I was done. I sighed. She sighed. I could almost hear her arms crossing in the back seat. And in the silence, as we drove down the freeway with the sun setting in the distance, a thought came to me.

"You know what?" I said.

"What?" she answered, sulking.

"I just realized, even when we have our differences, you and I are still more the same than we are different."

She didn't say anything. "And I think the fact that we disagree sometimes might be good."

"Why?" Her voice softened. (Was that the sound of her arms uncrossing?)

"Because I see your determination. You've got a strong will, and you can do a lot of great things with that in life."

"Hmm," was all she said.

We drove along, maybe another five minutes or so, and then . . .

"Mommy?"

"What?"

"I love you."

It totally took me by surprise. "I love you too," I told her.

"Thank you for taking me to swim tonight."

I smiled. "You're welcome."

Be More Blissful: What has been your "glimmer of sweetness" today? Take note and point it out to your kids, then think about how you can help create more moments like that. If you let yourself get caught up in stress and you reacted in a way you regret today, think about what you can do differently next time. And don't forget to give yourself grace; it paves the way for more glimmers of sweetness.

And that one small moment—that glimmer of sweetness—reminded me that even though some days parenting is hard, it's still good. The key is remembering to look for the good! When we do that, we not only keep the challenges of parenting from stealing our joy, we help our kids look for the good as well.

I know this example of Katie and me in the car is just one small situation. And believe me, I know parenting isn't always made up of moments that end so nicely. Sometimes, they end up in chaos and craziness. But that doesn't mean we can't control our reactions. That doesn't mean we can't love, even when it's difficult.

I remember one time when the kids were younger and Mike and I were heading out of town for the weekend. We were on our way to my mom and dad's house to drop the kids off, and as we were driving our wedding song came on the radio.

Thinking about the weekend ahead, and already excited about having time alone with Mike (no interruptions, no sibling rivalry, no noise . . .), I looked over at him and said, "How perfect to kick the weekend off with this song."

"What song?" Katie asked from the back seat, stopping the game of stuffed-animal-tug-of-war she'd been playing with Luke.

"This is the song Daddy and I had for our first dance at our wedding," I said, turning the radio up.

John Michael Montgomery sang . . . "And I like the way your eyes dance when you laugh . . ."

"Will I have to dance at my wedding?" Luke asked,

making a face.

"No, but by the time you get married, you'll probably want to." I smiled and settled back in to listen. "We should watch our wedding video this weekend," I told Mike. He reached over and grabbed my hand.

"If you sent your wedding video to *America's Funniest Home Videos* and won money for it, could you buy me a new spy kit?" Luke asked out of the blue. Not wanting to get into a conversation about a spy kit (I had a *song* to listen to), I humored him, "Sure," I said, thinking about my wedding day, and that first dance . . .

Out of the corner of my eye, I saw the kids start pulling on each other's animals again. And then, "Mom! She pulled the thread out of Chestnut's ear! Now it's hanging!" Luke screamed. I turned around. One of his stuffed dog's ears was longer than the other.

"I didn't mean to," Katie said. "It was an accident! We were playing!"

Luke reached over to grab her bear. "I'm gonna get Brownie's ear too!"

"Guys!" I said. "Leave each other's animals alone. And be quiet." I wanted to hear the last part of the song.

"Mom? Mom?! If you were me, would you pull Chestnut's other ear to match, or would you fix this one?" Luke went on, "Which do you think would look better?"

"Either way," I said, not even turning around. "No more questions! I'm trying to listen to this song!"

"Do you think I should pull the other ear?" I heard him ask Katie.

"I would," she said. "Here, let me see it."

"No!"

"Just let me see it."

"No! He's mine!"

And then there were stuffed animals flying in the back seat.

"If you guys don't stop throwing those around," Mike said, "I'm taking them and putting them in the front. I'm trying to drive." For a short minute, all was quiet. Except for the last part of our song. Which I relished. But as soon as it was over, Chestnut and Brownie flew up in the air again. "That's it," Mike said. "Hand them up here." And somehow I started our romantic weekend with two stuffed animals on my lap.

Not exactly sweetness, right? These kinds of moments definitely aren't bliss. And sometimes loving in the middle of the chaos is easier said than done. But the hard times do pass, the difficult phases our kids go through do eventually end, and before we know it, we turn around to reflect . . . and our kids are grown up.

I know that might be hard to imagine, especially if you are in the middle of a tough phase or challenging situation with your kids right now. I know it can be hard to stay positive, keep your patience, and stay calm. But our attitude and the way we look at the challenges we are facing not only determine how we respond to our kids and the kind of environment we create in our families, but also how we feel as a mom. The way we view our kids can have a huge impact as well. Let me explain.

Our pastor—a dad to three grown kids—has always

described the teenage years as glorious. Even when his kids were all teens at one time, he used that description when he talked about them. Glorious. It's not the typical word you hear when people talk about teenagers, right?

Every time he said it, I clung to the word, hoping it would hold true for my kids when they got to that age . . . hoping they wouldn't make some of the same mistakes I made, or do some of the things I did. And as I've entered the years of being a mom to a teenager, I've held that lens (firmly!) in front of me—the perspective that teenagers are glorious. And you know what? I'm finding that it's true. And I'm also finding that the way we view our kids plays a part in how we treat them, and how they act.

When Katie hit her pre-teens, things felt especially challenging. It seemed like she had gone from worshiping the ground I walk on to being irritated simply by my presence. Instead of Mommy, I became Mother. And as she desperately tried to find new freedoms, I held on, tighter than ever.

"Okay, Lord, I need help," I remember praying one day, totally discouraged. Not long after that, when I was at the library combing the shelves for an audio book for a long drive, my prayer was answered. A book called *For Parents Only—Getting Inside the Head of Your Kid* by Shaunti Feldhahn and Lisa A. Rice jumped out at me. I checked it out and started listening to it that day. Before I even finished, my heart was softened in a whole new way for teens.

Instead of feeling frustrated, I had compassion for all that Katie was going through—the changes, the social situations, the tug of war between staying a little girl and growing into a woman. And I was reminded of that time in my life—a time when so many things are new and exciting, yet scary and intimidating. A time when all you want to do is fit in.

I thought about my responses to her too, and it made me realize I was being more strict than understanding, more impatient than compassionate, and more critical than supportive. I decided to take her out to dinner and talk to her.

We sat down . . . and I apologized.

That's how I started the conversation: acknowledging that things had been rough between us for the past few months, and apologizing for my part. I shared that, just like becoming a teenager was new to her, parenting a teenager was new to me.

Her eyes softened. Her defensive posture dissolved. And she looked at me, hopeful . . . listening. I told her how proud I was of her—of who she was, and who she was becoming. And instead of pointing out things I was frustrated with (which I felt like I had been doing so much of), I told her all the things she was doing well— her grades, her choices with friends, her good work ethic, the way she helps people.

We talked about other things too: the reasons behind our rules and making sure she had a chance to ask questions. It opened new doors for discussion, and it was a great conversation. And somehow, in that hour, a healing took place. Maybe it was because she felt understood. Or maybe it was because she realized I'm learning right along with her. Or maybe it was simply because I said *sorry*. Whatever the reason, later that night, as I told her goodnight and was about to leave her room, she stopped me.

"Mommy?" she said in a soft voice.

Mommy.

I paused by the door. "Yes?"

"I love you." I could see her smiling in the dim light.

"I love you too," I said. I left her room feeling a little choked up, knowing that what our pastor said really is true. Teenagers *are* glorious. Sometimes, they just need to be reminded that they are. And sometimes as parents, we need to be reminded that the way we view our kids, the way we interact with them, and what we say and do, especially when they are being difficult, can shape the outcome. Loving, even when it's difficult, can pave the way for that love—and that bliss—to grow.

Mom-to-Mom: When do you find it most difficult to love? Can you think of a time this past week where you could've chosen to react differently? What happened?

Heart-to-Heart: "A gentle answer turns away wrath, but a harsh word stirs up anger."
—*Proverbs 15:1 NIV*

Are your answers usually gentle?

A Mom's Prayer: *God, help me to love, even when it's difficult. When I'm feeling less than equipped, or more than frustrated, remind me that You have all the answers, and that it doesn't all depend on me. Help me to look to You more, and myself less. Please give me the tools I need for the parenting challenges I'm facing right now. Help me to have a gentle answer in the middle of conflict and remind me to look for the good in all situations. Amen.*

Tip #5

Don't Worry, Be Happy
(or: Look for the lighter side; it's always there!)

"Every survival kit should include a sense of humor."
—Author Unknown

We all know the truth in the saying, "If Mama ain't happy, ain't nobody happy."

And any mom knows it's not always *easy* to be happy. We've all heard of moms (or maybe you're one of them) who can tell horror stories about finding furniture smeared with Vaseline or walls marked with ink. While I'm not saying you should throw your head back and laugh when these kinds of things happen, I am saying that these kinds of moments come with motherhood and the more we can look at the lighter side and not worry, the better off we'll be. And so will our kids.

One time when the kids were younger, they brought some frogs home from Grandma and Grandpa's house (my parents live on forty acres of beautiful land, which is home to plenty of frogs). It was my fault, actually—I told Katie and Luke they could bring them home. But I distinctly remember saying they could bring *two* frogs.

They brought *six*.

I could've intervened, but when they got home and took the lid off the bucket and I saw how tiny the frogs were, I figured, two or six; what's the difference? They were actually pretty cute. And, besides, it wasn't the frogs that were the problem. It was the crickets. A couple days after the frogs came home, Mike woke me up with a shake and a, "Gen, I'm sorry, but I have a meeting I can't be late for and there are crickets all over the house."

Crickets? It took me a second to figure out what he was saying. See, we'd bought this thing for the frogs called the Bug Box. It was a whole cricket ecosystem, all in one box. According to the label, "Tasty, plump morsels that stay fresh, too." And when it was time to feed the frogs, all you had to do was open the trap door on the box, shake a cricket out, and close the door. At least that's what *I* did before I set the box on our kitchen counter (I didn't read the instructions). I even taped over it for good measure.

Apparently, crickets eat tape. After they escaped, they proceeded to gallivant around our kitchen. And our living room. And our dining room. I don't know how many crickets came inside the Bug Box, but let me just say there was a great turnout at the six a.m. cricket party at our house that morning. There I was, on my hands and knees (without coffee, I might add), chasing crickets around with a paper towel and tossing them into the frog cage. Except for the crickets that were too fast or too big. Those I might've pinched a little too hard.

It was definitely one of those not-so-funny moments. But when Katie and Luke woke up and I told them about it, they cracked up. Luke couldn't wait to get to school and tell his friends. For a second-grade boy—his age at the time—you can bet he loved sharing that story.

And here's the thing: the whole episode was a pain

and the crickets were gross, but finding the humor and looking at the lighter side really did help. And you know what? Once you start doing that, the more you realize the benefit. Especially in the times you forget. Like the time we had to deal with mice in our house.

Mike and I bought Luke a mouse for his seventh birthday and right after that, Katie started building a case as to why *she* should get one too. "They get *lonely* by themselves, Mommy." Long story short: I gave in. The kids named their mice Spot and Blackberry and instantly fell in love. But one morning not too long after that, Katie screamed, "Mommmmy! Blackberry's gaaaaaawn!"

"She can't be gone," I said, running upstairs, hoping I was right. But, when I checked the cage, only Spot was in there. The door was open and Blackberry was gone. Somewhere. In. Our. House.

My mind raced: What if she'd been running around all night? What if we can't find her and she dies and then we *do* find her? I flew into action. "Hurry! Search your room!" I'm sad to say I didn't immediately see the lighter side of the situation. I wasn't the picture of calm; I was a wild woman. "Look in the closets and under the beds! This is *serious!*"

Katie began to panic, too. "*Poooor* Blackberry!" We ran from room to room, her on the verge of tears, and me on the verge of hysteria. But when we went into the laundry room, we saw wood shavings chewed off from the bottom of the door and I was relieved. I didn't even care (at the time) what the door looked like. What mattered was we found Blackberry. Or, by the looks of things, where she'd been all night.

I searched under the washer and dryer. Then I eyed the basket of laundry—the *clean* laundry waiting to be folded. Sure enough, after lifting a few things out, Blackberry crawled out from under a shirt. "Oh, Blackberry!" Katie laughed. "You're *sooo* cute! And *sooo* smart!" She picked her up and smiled. "Isn't she smart, Mommy?"

Well.

That wasn't the word *I* would've chosen right then. But I was glad we found her. And I was even happier to put her back in the cage. Only after it was all said and done did I realize how stressed I'd gotten and how it had fueled Katie's emotions. I also realized I could've handled it differently. And by Blackberry's fifth escape (yes, fifth), I found myself laughing and saying, "Don't worry; she'll turn up." And she always did.

With each situation that happens, we have a choice as moms to handle it positively or negatively. We have a choice to stress out or take it in stride. In that situation with Katie's mouse, I wasn't the example of calm, but in the times where I have remembered to look at the lighter side and not worry, it has definitely helped. Our kids follow our lead, and when we embrace the adventures of motherhood and the mishaps that come with it, we're not only more blissful, we set a positive example for our kids in handling the not-so-funny moments in their lives too.

And that may be the biggest benefit of all.

Mom-to-mom: When was the last not-so-funny moment you experienced? How did you handle it? Could having a sense of humor or not worrying have changed the outcome?

Heart-to-Heart: "Be joyful always."
—1 Thessalonians 5:16 GNT

Are there certain things that tend to steal your joy? What are they and how can you prevent that from happening?

A Mom's Prayer: *God, help me to be more joyful today. Help me to laugh and see the lighter side of things. If I've gotten too serious lately, restore my sense of humor. I want to show my kids how to handle the stress of life in a positive way and I want to set an example that helps them navigate tough times in their own lives. Thank you that I'm never alone and that You are always by my side to strengthen me. Thank you also that You will never give me more than I can handle. I look forward to finding the joy in every single moment today! Amen.*

Tip #6

Relax
(or: You won't ruin your kids if you lighten up every now and then!)

"Good humor and laughter are far too wonderful
not to come straight from the heart of God."
—Beth Moore

When the kids were about seven and nine, Mike got new phones for our house that made working at home easier for him. One of the features of the phones was that they could intercom each other—a great thing if you needed to ask a question from upstairs or downstairs and didn't want to yell. Katie thought it was great, too, and had a ton of fun calling from room to room. Especially at bedtime.

One night, literally a minute after we put the kids to bed, the intercom started . . . *Beep. Beep. Beep.* I picked up the phone. "Mommy?" she asked in a cute little voice. "Can I have some warm milk?"

"No, Honey. It's late," I told her. "You haven't even *tried* to get to sleep yet."

"But, Mommy, I'm *starving.*"

"You already had dinner and brushed your teeth. It's time for bed." I went to hang the phone up.

"Wait. Mommy?"

"What?"

"If I have crackers, do I have to brush my teeth again?"

"You can't have crackers."

"But I'm *starving*."

I knew I should stand firm. I *knew* it. But against my better judgment, I started to waver. *Maybe she's going through a growth spurt*, I thought. *Maybe she should have a little snack . . .* "All *right*," I said, guiltily aware of the fact that I was teaching her if she bugged me long enough, I'd give in. "You can have an apple."

"Mommy?"

"*What?*"

"What about quesadillas?"

I'd just caved and offered her a snack, and now she was getting picky? "You can't have *quesadillas*. It's time for *bed*," I told her. "I'm hanging up the phone and I'm bringing you some apples."

"Okay. But, Mommy?" she asked in her sweetest voice possible.

"*What?*"

"Can you please cook me some bacon?"

Bacon?!

"No! I'm not making bacon. It's nine o'clock. What do you think this is? *Room service?*"

Cute little laugh. "Yeah."

I know I should've stopped the conversation right there. Or given her a consequence. Or done *something* to discourage her behavior. But, blame it on being at that delirious parental breaking point where, like it or not, you're either going to laugh or cry, I started cracking up. I couldn't believe she was asking me to cook her bacon at nine at night. And she was *serious*. I laughed, then she laughed, then we both laughed so hard we couldn't stop.

"Well, it's *not*," I finally managed, catching my breath.

"Okay," she said, still giggling.

"I'll cut you some strawberries if you don't want apples." I tried to sound firm. "Then you *need to go to sleep*."

"Okay. I'll have strawberries."

"Okay."

Sigh.

"And Mommy?" she said.

"What?!"

"While you're at it, can you make me some warm milk?"

After that night, I didn't think those intercoms were such a great feature after all. But laughing and relaxing about the whole thing *did* help the situation. Even though Katie shouldn't have been calling me for a snack via personal delivery, and I shouldn't have caved like I did, laughing ended up being so much better than getting mad and yelling. And that one night of me giving in to her requests didn't teach her to demand a snack every night. It didn't teach her to beg me until she got what she wanted, either. Honestly, she hasn't asked for quesadillas or bacon at night since! But she and I share a memory that we *still* laugh about together. She still asks if I remember "That one time I asked you for room service and we cracked up."

Be More Blissful: The next time you are in a frustrating or trying situation with your kids, stop and decide to handle it differently. Take a deep breath, say a prayer and ask God to help you relax, then hold that yell—and see what happens!

Ask yourself: how am I when faced with an unexpected challenge? A chaotic situation? An unpleasant surprise? Even if you know the challenge isn't a crisis, but instead something like spilled orange juice on the carpet or melted crayons in the car, these not-so-serious situations can still put you and your reactions to the test. Think about your first response as a mom when something like this comes your way, then think about if there is anything you can or should do differently in the way you react. Even if you don't plan for these types of situations ahead of time, you can still change how you react—and how you feel—when you're in the thick of things.

Almost every holiday over the years, we have rolled our barbeques out to the street in the court we live on and spent time with our neighbors. Whether it's Fourth of July, St. Patrick's Day, or just a three-day weekend, our neighborhood loves to get together. One Saturday, when Katie was about nine, we were getting ready to have one of our gatherings in the court and I decided to make cupcakes and brownies. Katie thought it would be helpful to surprise me and make them ahead of time—while

I was upstairs showering.

When I came downstairs and went into the kitchen, I found her working away happily—three different bowls of ingredients going on at once, and five—*five*—boxes of cake and brownie mix open and sitting on the counter. She even had cupcakes ready to go in the oven; they were overflowing out of the cupcake holders and onto the edges of the pan. It was one of those moments where you walk in the room and it takes you a minute to realize what's happening. And once you do realize, you have to be careful about your reaction. The kitchen was a disaster, and I literally had to pause and think about how I was going to respond.

"What are you doing?" I asked, trying to sound . . . ahem . . . pleased.

"I'm helping you," she said proudly.

Even though it was hard, I didn't say a word about the mess. I didn't dive in and start cleaning up after her. I didn't offer to help. Instead, I thanked her and let her finish. In other words, I forced myself to relax. And you know what? My relaxing was good for her, *and* for me. Sure, she took a while to clean up the kitchen after she was done, and, yes, we had to throw one batch of brownies out because it had a tad too much water in it, but the rest of the desserts turned out great. And she felt good about helping.

Which is what really matters, anyway, right?

Mom-to-Mom: What have been some moments lately where you could have relaxed more? How did you respond to what was happening at the time? Did it help or hurt the situation?

Heart-to-Heart: "Come to me, all you who are weary and burdened, and I will give you rest. Take my yoke upon you and learn from me, for I am gentle and humble in heart, and you will find rest for your souls. For my yoke is easy and my burden is light."
—*Matthew 11:28-30 NIV*

What are you carrying right now that feels heavy or is keeping you from relaxing? Sometimes we create and carry burdens that were never meant to be ours. Give your stress to God and feel the lightness only He can give.

A Mom's Prayer: *God, I can be so bad at remembering to relax sometimes! I get stressed or impatient, and I think everything depends on me. Help me to remember that Your burden is light. Thank you for being so patient with me and calling me (again and again) to a place of remembering your promises. Fill my heart and home with good humor and laughter. Amen.*

Tip #7

Create the Laugh
(Because being a mom is fun. Really.)

"You're never too old to do goofy stuff."
—Ward Cleaver from the TV show *Leave it to Beaver*

We've talked about how lightening up and relaxing can set a positive tone in your family. But there's more to humor and laughter than just responding. As moms, we have a huge opportunity to *create* the laugh, and in doing so, create an environment where joy can grow.

We've all heard the saying "laughter is good medicine." But sometimes mommy-hood is serious business, right? After all, we have to keep everyone on schedule, everyone organized and everyone fed. We have a house to manage and a gazillion things to do. Sometimes, having fun isn't the first priority on the to-do list. There are *kids* to raise for gosh sakes!

Don't get me wrong; I love a good laugh. But, I'm the first to admit; I sometimes forget to *create the fun* in the middle of our busy days. Mike's usually the one to wrestle the kids or start pillow fights. And *I'm* usually the one telling them to be careful or warning them that somebody's going to get hurt. But being a mom can do that to us, right?

Slow down. You might crash.
Don't climb. You might fall.

Be quiet.
Don't run.
Sit still.
Be gentle.

How many of you hear yourself in those words? I know I do. Why is it that parenthood can suddenly make us so serious? I once heard that adults laugh an average of fifteen times a day, while kids laugh an average of four hundred times. And while that makes me happy that kids are having so much fun, it makes me sad that maybe us moms aren't. And we should be. Studies have found that laughter may help prevent heart disease, reduce tension and stress, boost our immune system and reduce pain. And, for those of you who don't like to exercise, get this: laughter has even been found to be equivalent to small amounts of exercise because it massages internal organs in the body. Who knew!

There's no way around it: we moms need to laugh. We need to have more fun. I especially need to work on this one sometimes. A while ago when Mike and I and Katie and Luke were out running errands, Katie asked if I wanted to play Brain Quest. "Sure," I said, less than enthused.

She grabbed the game from under the back seat and flipped to her first question. "How do you spell one more than seventeen?"

"E-i-g-h-t-e-e-n," I yawned.

"Okay. Correct this sentence: Bill and I is going to the ball game."

"Bill and I *are* going to the ball game."

"What is the opposite of private?"

"Public."

Suddenly, she stopped. "Mommy," she said. "You're not playing it right. You have to be more fun when you answer, like Daddy."

She had a point and I knew it. Even though I was "playing" with her, I was half-heartedly answering the questions and not being much fun. So I decided to take her comment as a challenge. "Okay," I said perking up, "ask me another one."

And when she did, I gave the silliest, most obnoxious answer I could. Everyone started cracking up, including me. It was great to be reminded of the impact I can have in creating a fun environment for my family. As moms, we play such an important role in setting the tone and mood for our homes. And when we remember to be intentional about having fun and creating the laugh, it's easy to see the effect—not only on our families, but on our happiness as moms.

> **Be More Blissful: When was the last time you did something fun to create a laughable or fun moment with your kids? Write down one thing you can do this week to create more laughter for yourself and your family.**

Creating the laugh isn't just about remembering to be silly with our kids; it's also about deliberately creating opportunities where fun can flourish. When Katie was about nine, she and I set out one Saturday to run errands. I had a list of things to do and was looking forward to being productive. But a few minutes after leaving, when we neared the Starbucks around the corner, I thought of something: three times that week, she had asked if we could get a hot chocolate together. Three times I had said no. It was "We have to get to basketball," and "We have to get to swim team," and "We can't, or we'll be late for cheer."

As I thought about that, I decided to do something different. Our schedule was open, and I wanted to make the most of it. I smiled and looked in the rearview mirror. "Want to go to Starbucks? Just us girls?"

Her eyes got wide. "Sure!"

We sat at a table outside. As we ate, we sprinkled crumbs on the ground and watched the birds. We talked about how she was feeling about entering fourth grade, and what her favorite thing about the summer was. We saw a dog that reminded her of our dog Lady who had died a month before, and we talked about God and Heaven. We must've sat there for an hour, but I'm not sure.

I never checked the time.

After Starbucks, we headed to a store, where, halfway through the aisles, Katie discovered the massage chairs. "Mommy! We have to try these!" She hopped in one of the chairs and pushed the demo button, laughing as the rollers went up and down her back. Normally, I would've watched her for a few minutes and then hurried her along. But instead, I plopped down in the chair next to her and said, "All right. How do you turn this thing on?"

We sat there for a long time, laughing, and "oohing" and "ahhhing" through our massages. We even got a few stares from people walking by. Which made us laugh harder. And even though Katie and I didn't set out to do anything special, we ended up—in the middle of ordinary things—having an *extra*ordinary time together.

As moms, we don't have to make grand plans to create fun memories with our kids. We just need to be intentional, ignore the clock, and take the time to create space to have fun. When I think of all the times I've said "Not now" or "Wait until I'm done" to my kids, I still regret it. Yet I've never regretted the times I've stopped and had fun with them.

And it's amazing how *those* are often the times that an unexpected moment happens—a milestone or joyful memory—a moment that wouldn't have existed if we hadn't taken the time to create the laugh.

> **Be More Blissful: Clear something off your calendar today and see what your kids do with the free time. Record it with photos and talk about it afterwards. Who knows, you may just start a new tradition!**

Maybe for you, making time to create the laugh means letting the dishes wait, folding the laundry later, or running the errands tomorrow so you and your kids can go to the park or a movie together. And maybe that's hard for you. As someone who has a hard time walking by the couch without straightening the pillows, I know it's not always easy to let things go. But don't let keeping your house clean or other *to-dos* prevent you from setting aside fun time with your kids. Give yourself permission to have a day off, away from the house, and take your kids on an adventure. Once you start recognizing how easy it can be to create fun moments with your kids— once you start being intentional about creating the time to laugh—it becomes a happy habit. Having fun as a mom—having fun in *life*, for that matter—is so much about just making it happen. And when you do that, you not only create the laugh in your family, you create space for bliss to blossom. And, believe me, it does.

Mom-to-Mom: When was the last time you did something out-of-the-norm to create a laughable or fun moment with your kids? Write down one thing you can do this week to have fun with them, then make sure to do it!

Heart-to-Heart: "Our mouths were filled with laughter, our tongues with songs of joy. Then it was said among the nations, 'The Lord has done great things for them.'"
—*Psalm 126:2 NIV*

Is your home filled with laughter? Take a minute to remember the great things God has done for you, be re-filled with joy, and be intentional about sharing that joy with your kids.

A Mom's Prayer: *God, help me to create an environment in my home where laughter comes easily and often. Help me to think of opportunities for fun and let these opportunities not just come as ideas, but be something I carry forward and do. Thank you for all the laughter I've known as a mom, and thank you for the fun memories we've had in our family. Help me to set an example of joy and enthusiasm in my home. I pray that my children will have a passion for life and find joy in all that they do. Amen.*

Tip #8

Say Yes
(Because sometimes there's no reason to say no!)

"Think big thoughts, but relish small pleasures."
—H. Jackson Brown, Jr., *Life's Little Instruction Book*

Sometimes, turning our ordinary days into blissful ones can be as simple as saying yes to things we would normally say no to.

When Luke and Katie were younger, they loved building forts. I don't know about you, but the blankets, pillows, chairs, and sometimes even umbrellas they would use to build their castles, aren't exactly my favorite things to have taking up the family room. And to top it off, they'd usually want to leave their fort up for days, which is exactly what they did the time they built a fort out of an oversized umbrella and a huge pink blanket in our front room.

At the time, I was reading the inspirational book, *One Month to Live,* by Chris and Kerry Shook, and it was a good thing I was. Because every fiber in me wanted to tell my kids to *hurry up and get that pink-igloo-umbrella-thing cleaned up and put away.*

But when they asked if they could leave it up, I stopped and thought, if I truly had one month to live, would I care?

So I said they could leave it, despite the fact that it was in the first room you see when you walk in the door, and despite the fact that a little while turned into a week (and a bunch of friends and neighbors even stopped by).

But you know what?

I learned that the house doesn't always have to be matchy-matchy and perfect. To be honest, it was a whole lot more fun with a big pink fort in the front room. It made for some good conversation, and being able to leave it up day after day surprised my kids in a really fun way. Sometimes as moms, we are quick to say no to things (I know I'm guilty of this) when there really is no reason not to say yes. But if we try to be more aware of that, and even say yes more often, the unexpected can happen: unexpected surprises, unexpected memories, unexpected laughter, unexpected . . . bliss.

> **Be More Blissful: Make it a point to say yes today to something you would normally say no to, and see what happens!**

I know you might be reading this and thinking that saying yes to kids is not always as easy as leaving a fort up. Some of the things kids ask aren't exactly convenient. It can be hard to stop everything and say yes to things like "Can we go to a movie?" or "Can we walk to the park?" when the schedule is packed and you're running from one place to another. I've been there. *So* been there! But sometimes, it's in the thick of that busyness that we can see the value of saying yes the most.

When Katie was younger, she joined a cheerleading

squad. It was our first experience with cheer and I didn't realize when we signed up what a commitment it would be. (For those of you who are familiar with this sport, I was obviously clueless.) Luke was in select soccer at the time, so we were really busy with practices for both kids several times a week.

During the last few weeks of that summer, I became acutely aware of how quickly the summer months had passed with us rushing around from one sport and activity to the next. I longed for a few days where my kids could play in the yard, eat popsicles, make a lemonade stand . . . and just do *summer* things. So I decided I wanted to end the summer in a more relaxed way. I really wanted Katie and Luke to experience carefree, summer fun before the school year started. I wanted them to play outside and sleep in . . . and just be kids.

And, by deliberately setting aside time and clearing our calendar so we had nowhere to go and nothing to do, *kids they were.* As we set out to literally just do nothing, it was fun to see how the kids filled the time—with drawing and crafts and playing games and having fun. Luke emptied most of the kitchen cupboards one day and conducted experiments in our salad spinner, mixing shampoo with water and swirling it around. And, of course, adding a pen cap, a string, and a piece of plastic in the spinner makes an "extra-powerful tornado, Mom!"

Katie, on the other hand, instead of putting the dishes away as she emptied the dishwasher one morning, built a mini-pyramid out of bowls and cups on the counter. And that's pretty much how our whole week was, filled with one interesting project after another.

We cleaned out Katie's room and moved her furniture, and when she told me she wanted her bed at an angle right in the middle of her room, I surprised myself and said . . . why not? It wasn't the plan I had—her bed nice and tidy against the wall—but it looked cute the way she wanted it. And it felt good for me to just *let go and let be.*

When the kids asked if they could swim in their socks, I surprised myself again and said yes, because, really, why not? I even joined them in the pool and did a cannon ball into the deep end and got my hair wet. Katie and Luke were so excited they practically drowned me. But to see their faces and how happy they were made the blow-drying-my-hair-all-over-again-in-the-middle-of-the-day worth it. (Which, by the way, isn't vanity. It's necessity. If you have hair that frizzes when it air-dries, you understand.)

It was a fun, off-the-wall, and messy week. I did things I don't normally do. I said yes to things I would've normally said no to. The house was a disaster and, to be honest, I got burnt-out on paint brushes, glue guns, games, and projects. But I learned what a positive impact letting go and saying yes can have.

On my kids *and* on me.

Mom-to-Mom: Do you tend to be a *yes* person or a *no* person? Why do you think that is? Have you said yes to something lately that lead to a fun memory or special time with your kids?

Heart-to-Heart: "In their hearts humans plan their course, but the Lord establishes their steps."
—Proverbs 16:9 NIV

Are you planning every detail of your day today, or are you open to God's leading? Sometimes, we just need to drop our plans and be willing to say yes and follow!

A Mom's Prayer: *God, please help me be more spontaneous and say yes to my kids when there is no reason to say no. I want to live freely and easily. I want to soak in Your joy and have it spill over into my parenting. Please let my kids see Your light in my eyes and hear Your voice in my laughter. Let the yeses that I say open the door for my kids to see the endless possibilities in life. Amen.*

Tip #9

Get Back to the Basics
(And just love simply.)

"Simplicity is ultimately a matter of focus."
—Ann Voskamp, author of *One Thousand Gifts:
A Dare to Live Fully Right Where You Are*

I remember so many moments of bliss I experienced right after Katie and Luke were born: sitting in the rocker with each of them, holding their miniature hands, marveling at their tiny feet, sometimes being overwhelmed at how precious they were. It was all so miraculous, amazing, and wonderful. If only there was a way to keep things so magical, right?

But there *is* one thing that helps us get back to the basics and recapture that bliss, and it has everything to do with being grateful. A grateful heart *is* a blissful heart. Somehow, when we view motherhood as the gift that it is, chaos and all, our hearts shift from stressed to thankful, and it's a whole lot easier to get caught up in the joy.

Believe me; I've had to work on this one. Gratitude is a daily choice. I'm the first to admit that I can hurry through a whole day forgetting to be thankful for what's in front of me. It's a discipline I've had to work on and grow in, and I know from experience that the more thankful I am, the healthier and happier I feel. There's a fun exercise I heard about a while ago that helped me to really think about being more grateful as a mom. The challenge was to describe motherhood in six words.

Here was my attempt (because, really, can you put it into six?): *Heartstrings connected for all eternity. Grateful.*

Even though it was just an exercise, it forced me to simplify—to stop and think about what really matters . . . my love for my Katie and Luke and how grateful I am to be their mom. If you stop and think about how amazing motherhood is—*truly* think about it—and focus on being grateful, you realize, even though parenting is definitely not simple, the love that comes with it is.

> "You don't really understand human nature
> unless you know why a child on a
> merry-go-round will wave at his parents
> every time around—and why his parents
> will always wave back."
> —William D. Tammeus

As a mom, I know you totally get this quote. You understand why you wave every time your child goes around . . . and around. Even if it's the twentieth time, and even if you're tired and ready to leave, as long as your child waves at you, you wave back. And you keep waving until the merry-go-round stops. Because that's love.

That's simple love.

> **Be More Blissful:** Look for the bliss-moments today: your baby's smile, a hug from your toddler, lunch with your teenager, a call from your oldest away at college. Don't let the moment pass without taking notice and whispering a prayer of thanks. The more you start thanking, the more thankful you will feel.

Loving simply isn't just about being grateful though. It's also about loving unconditionally—no strings attached. Years ago, when Katie first started doing swim team, we were at one of her meets and I caught the last part of another age group's race. All the swimmers had finished except for one girl in the middle lane. She was struggling with her backstroke, was halfway through her lap, and the crowd had quieted. All eyes were on her.

But there was one voice that could still be heard. Alongside the pool, this girl's dad walked at the same pace she swam. "You can do it!" he said, clapping. "Keep going!" You could tell he was proud that even though his daughter was having a hard time, she wasn't giving up. It didn't matter to him that the other swimmers had already finished. And it didn't matter that his child would come in last. What mattered was that his daughter knew he believed in her.

He wasn't sitting in the bleachers, disappointed or frustrated. He was by his daughter's side, proudly cheering her on. And when she finished, he beamed. "Good job!" He smiled. It reminded me what simple, unconditional love looks like. I think as parents we sometimes get so caught up in wanting our kids to *do good* that we worry too much what others think. We don't mean to, but we might attach conditions to how we love. We might get too caught up in wanting our kids to succeed, or focus more on the competition than whether or not our kids are having fun or building character. Maybe we forget sometimes, trying *is* winning.

There have been times I've caught myself wanting *my* child to score that winning goal. Or make that basket. Or get all A's on that report card. Or get the lead role in the school play. I'm not saying it's bad to want our kids to excel. Most of the time, I think our desire to see our kids succeed simply comes from wanting the best for them. Whether it's in school, in sports, or in *life*.

And I'm not saying that winning is bad either. It's not; it's exciting. We *should* teach our kids to reach for goals. And to try hard. And to learn how to apply themselves. But there's a balance to be found. If our kids are giving their best effort, should it matter if they come in last? And what good is first place if they only push themselves for our approval? A loss every now and then just might build more character than an undefeated season.

Whether our kids come in first place or last, whether they win or lose, they should know without a doubt that we love them. We can practice tough love if grades are suffering or our kids are slacking in some area of their life, but they should never feel like our love for them is tied to their performance. And even though we expect our kids to know that we love them no matter what they do or how they behave, sometimes our actions or words don't communicate that to them.

When Katie and Luke decided they wanted to get baptized several years ago, I brought them to meet with the leader of our children's ministry (standard practice to prepare them and make sure they understood what baptism meant). We met in the church nursery, all of us sitting in the sliding rockers that were used on the weekends. As the ministry leader began to talk, Luke started rocking back and forth in his chair. His eyes wandered, and the rocking escalated.

I leaned over and whispered in his ear, "Stop rocking and look her in the eyes when she's talking to you."

She smiled sweetly at Luke. Evidently, I hadn't whispered quietly enough. "That might bother your mom, Sweetie, but it's okay with me. It's hard to sit in these rockers and not rock." She winked at me. Luke smiled and instantly seemed more relaxed and comfortable.

And I realized I'd been more worried about how he was acting than the conversation that was taking place. More worried about his performance than what was going on with his character. So for the rest of the meeting, I kept quiet. When he slouched in his chair, I didn't tell him to sit up. When his eyes wandered around the room again, I bit my tongue.

And a funny thing happened as I kept silent.

My normally shy Luke completely opened up. Free to relax without me correcting him, he ended up engaging in the conversation about baptism, and then sharing an unrelated story about something that had happened earlier that day with a couple of boys who had said something mean to him.

Our ministry leader finished the meeting by praying with Luke about the boys. And later that night, Luke prayed for them again, all on his own. And I couldn't help but wonder . . . if I had continued to correct him in the meeting, would he have opened up and shared the story? Would he have prayed like that?

It was a powerful reminder how, sometimes, when we're able to take a step back and let go of our expectations, when we are able to remove the "conditions" of our love, when we are able to just love simply, amazing things can happen.

And simple is always blissful, moms.

Mom-to-Mom: What are you most thankful for as a mom right now?

Heart-to-Heart: "Dear friends, let us love one another, for love comes from God."
—1 John 4:7 NIV

Parenting can seem so complicated sometimes. But I love this advice from one of my friends: "When in doubt, just love them." Sounds pretty simple, doesn't it? And what an awesome reminder that love comes from God. How can we accept this amazing gift of love and not pass it to others, simply and *unconditionally?*

A Mom's Prayer: *God, thank you for the way You love me, no matter what. Help me to love my kids and my family that way too. I want them to know that my love for them isn't tied to their performance, but that I love them for who they are. When parenting gets hard and things get crazy, please remind me that all I need to do is remember how much You love me, and then pour that love into my kids. Amen.*

Tip #10

Love, for Real
(Because we're all on the same team.)

"It is astonishing how little one feels alone
when one loves."
—John Bulwer

There's a small group of men who meet in the coffee shop where I often write. They sit there—the three of them huddled together—at a table by the window. The same men, the same table, the same ceramic mugs that they bring themselves, every time.

The all have gray hair, weathered skin, and deep laugh lines. I'll admit; I've listened to their conversations. It's hard not to. They sit together and talk with a sense of familiarity that makes you want to know what they're saying and how they came to be such good friends. Their conversations are sprinkled with nods and laughter as they share stories, ask each other questions, and catch up on each other's lives.

Every so often, one of them will talk quietly—too quietly for other people in the coffee shop to hear—and by the way the other two men lean in with a look of concern on their faces, you know they're discussing something serious, maybe even sad. But you also know, just by watching them, that whatever the burden may be, it is lighter when they leave, because they've spent time together.

It's like that with us as moms, too. When we get together and share what we're going through, it's hard to feel alone. Yet sometimes, being intentional about spending time with other moms isn't always easy. Sometimes, we're so exhausted or busy, that meeting at a coffee shop and sitting around chatting seems like an impossibility. And, besides, who's going to watch the kids, right?

And then there are the walls we put up. Do you ever feel like you can't share what you are really going through, so you keep it inside? Do you ever feel like you are the only one struggling with parenting, or the only who whose kids don't listen to you, or the only one who is frustrated with your marriage lately? I promise you mom, you aren't. And by spending time with other moms and being real and vulnerable with each other, you come to know that. And you also have the opportunity to encourage and lift each other up.

I know that when you look at the quote at the beginning of this chapter, you might think that's all you do as a mom—love others. You love your husband, your kids, your kids' teachers, your kids' friends, your neighbors, your families . . . the list goes on and on. But even though some days it might sound good to *be* alone, it's never good to *feel* alone. Notice how the quote doesn't say "when loved"? It says when one *loves*—when you are the one doing the loving. When we take the time to be with others and love, for real—to be authentic about what we are going through, to share our struggles and invite others to do the same, and to love each other without judgment, the benefit and blessing comes back to *us*. How joyful you feel as a mom has so much to do with the relationships you have with others.

Study after study that has looked at the cause of a person's happiness has found that relationships and connection with others both rise to the top as predicting factors. You would think this would be good news for us moms since, like I mentioned, we are always *loving others*. But in our day-to-day role as parents, we can still feel isolated. Weeks, even months, can pass in a blur without us even feeling like we've come up for air. We can be surrounded by our kids, our husbands, our families, yet we might still feel alone and overwhelmed.

If you're in that place, I encourage you to open yourself up to other moms. Join a moms group, meet with friends at a park with the kids, or simply make a phone call to another mom that you know. When you take that step to let your walls down and build community, it can replace that feeling of isolation with joy.

Be More Blissful: Whatever you are going through or feeling as a mom right now, you're not alone. Being honest and vulnerable with others helps you know that. Reach out to one other mom today and either share something you are struggling with, or ask her if you can help her in any way. Then see the joy unfold!

And this is where loving for real comes in—being honest, compassionate, and vulnerable. As we reach out and connect with other moms, we need to be real in our relationships. An empty or inauthentic friendship isn't going to lead to happiness. We need to offer each other compassion and understanding, not judge one another.

I had a conversation with a mom a while ago that really made me think about this. She was worried about her two-year-old, who had become a picky eater. Frustrated with meal-time battles and the fact that her daughter had just learned the word no, this mom threw her hands up and said, "My husband and I decided we're failing as parents." It broke my heart. Anybody who has had a two-year-old knows that these types of battles are totally normal. I understood this mom's frustration, because I've been there.

As I was telling her that, she said, "I don't know. Maybe I should join a mom's group or something. I don't usually talk about this kind of stuff." I could see the relief she felt in sharing, and I agreed, telling her how much mom's groups helped me, especially during those first few years. "I'm not sure, though," she said. "I just feel like any mom groups I've heard about have been judgmental and negative."

That broke my heart too. But, I think it's safe to say we've all been guilty of judging other moms at some point. I remember when I was at the doctor's office one time picking up medicine for Katie when she had strep throat, another mom, about eight and a half months pregnant, sat near me, looking completely exhausted. Her daughter (about two) clung to her leg, coughing and crying, and her son (about four) ran around the waiting room.

When the little girl's cries got louder and the mom didn't respond, people in the waiting room began to stare. I could almost hear them thinking, *Why isn't that mom doing something?*

After several minutes, the mom tiredly leaned over and picked the little girl up. Suddenly, the crying stopped . . . and her daughter threw up. *Everywhere.* There was an audible gasp in the room. And plenty more stares. I hurried to the counter, grabbed the Kleenex off the nurse's station, and brought it back to the mom, whose look of appreciation gave me a lump in my throat. I could feel her embarrassment and exhaustion. I could feel the irritation in the room too, as if it was the mom's fault her daughter got sick.

I felt so sorry for this mom, and I hated the fact that others seemed so irritated with her. But, I have to admit, there have been times *I* was the one doing the judging. When Katie was born, Mike and I started off parenting with a six-week parenting class. We read a bunch of books and tried to get as many tools under our belt as we could. And as Katie became a toddler and started to test us, she didn't get away with much (the poor first child). We implemented what we learned and were pretty happy with the results. Up to that point, when I would see other kids throwing a tantrum and the mom not doing anything about it, I'd sometimes wonder, *Why is the mom allowing that? Why isn't she doing X, Y, or Z?* In other words, I judged.

Then there was that fateful day in Target when Katie was about two and a half (just old enough to start having some real tantrums of her own) and she threw herself prostrate on the floor, kicking and screaming. No matter what I did, no matter what *X, Y,* or *Z* consequence I promised, there was no stopping her. It was humbling, to say the least. I got more than a few stares as I carried her out of the store, me hot-flashing with embarrassment and her kicking wildly. Ever since then, when I see kids acting out like that, I *feel* for the mom instead of judging her. Because I've been there. We've *all* been there at one point or another, no matter how well we discipline or how many parenting books we read.

Every child is different and every mom is different, and what works for one parent or child may not work for another. And sometimes, yes, we mess up. We *don't* handle situations the way we should, or we *aren't* consistent. *Still.* Let's not judge each other. We come from different walks of life, backgrounds, and families. If we've perfected our kids' nap schedules, we shouldn't judge moms who drive their kids around so they'll fall asleep in the car. And if we don't think a nap schedule is important, we shouldn't judge moms who do. If our kids go to public school, we shouldn't judge moms who home school. And if we home school, we shouldn't judge moms who don't. The list could go on and on.

We're different people with different reasons for the decisions we make, or have to make. *But we're all moms.* And we're in this together. Motherhood is hard enough without the judging stares or whispers from others that make us feel like we're failing. So the next time we see a mom struggling or handling a situation differently than we would, instead of judging, let's love for real. Let's help her, or smile at her, or pray for her, or encourage her.

If we all did that, just think how much easier being a mom would become.

Mom-to-Mom: Do you feel like you can be real with other moms or do you hold back? What is the biggest challenge you have right now in communicating with other moms or sharing your struggles?

Heart-to-Heart: "Do not judge, or you too will be judged. For in the same way you judge others, you will be judged, and with the measure you use, it will be measured to you. Why do you look at the speck of sawdust in your brother's eye and pay no attention to the plank in your own eye?"
—Matthew 7:1-3 NIV

Have you ever felt judged as a mom? Have you ever been the one doing the judging? What was the result?

A Mom's Prayer: *God, You know how alone I feel sometimes. Help me to reach out to others and build more authentic relationships. Please bring another mom alongside me who I can confide in, or who I can encourage. Help me to not be so hard on myself, or others. Let words of encouragement flow through me. Help me to be open and* *real with others, and help me to see all the good in the moms in my life—in my mom, my mother-in-law, my sister, my grandma, myself, and in the friends You have surrounded me with. Thank you for the way these moms have blessed me. Help me to become part of more mom communities, and help me to be a blessing back! Amen.*

Tip #11

Reach Out
(It leaves beautiful scars.)

"Hate leaves ugly scars, love leaves beautiful ones."
—Mignon McLaughlin

I've heard it said that people either like to cook or they like to bake, but they rarely like to do both. And for me, that's true. Cookies, cupcakes, biscuits . . . I love making them. Desserts for the holidays and cakes for birthdays? I love those too. There's nothing like a house filled with the smell of things like brownies or apple pie.

But cooking? That's another story.

It's not that I *don't* cook. I do. And it's not that I *hate* it, either. I don't. It's just that I always seem to get stuck in a rut, making the same six or seven recipes over and over. And every once in a while, when I happen to read a cooking magazine or see an amazing recipe online, panic sets in and I worry that I'm not cooking enough variety. So I get super-motivated and dig through my recipes and try something new, which, especially when the kids were younger, is sometimes received with a less-than-enthusiastic response.

Now that Katie and Luke are getting older, it's getting more fun to try new things and find new meals they like (if you have picky eaters, there's hope!). But when they were younger, they weren't always so happy when new food was put in front of them. I must've said "This isn't a restaurant" a million times.

In fact, when they were about seven and nine, I got so frustrated by their picky eating, and so worried that they weren't getting the variety in their diet that they needed, I put a plan in motion to help them try new foods. Every week, they were responsible for going through our recipe books, picking out one meal each that they wanted to try, then being the head cook for that meal during the week.

The plan worked. We found some new dinners that they really liked, and they tried foods that they probably wouldn't have tried if they weren't the ones who'd chosen them. But, I have to admit, after several weeks of doing this I began to feel the effort of it. The plan meant setting aside time to help them read through cookbooks. And longer trips to the store. And a messier kitchen on the nights they cooked. In other words, it was turning out to be a whole lot of work.

A while after we had been doing this, Mike and I took the kids to Starbucks one morning after church. We brought a couple cookbooks with us because we were heading to the grocery store afterwards and needed to pick out what we were going to make that week so we could get the ingredients. Katie and Luke flipped through the pages, looking at the pictures, asking questions, deciding . . .

and deciding . . .

and deciding . . .

until finally, they made their choices.

"Good job," I said, trying to sound enthusiastic.

"These are going to be *great*." I marked the pages and smiled, but inside I groaned as I scanned the long list of ingredients.

And that's when the woman at the table next to us stood up and came over. She put her hand on my back and leaned down. "You're a good mom," she said.

I smiled, confused. "Thanks," I told her.

"Is this something you do all the time? With the cookbooks?" she asked.

I didn't know she'd heard us. I explained what we were doing with the cookbooks, and why.

She patted my back again and said, "I think that's great." Then she repeated, "You're a really good mom."

And to be honest with you, I almost started bawling right there in Starbucks. I was so impacted by the way that woman reached out to me because I was at a point where I was starting to wonder if all the effort was worth it. And I needed to be reminded that it was. Her sweet words were affirmation to me that sometimes the more time-consuming or inconvenient choice for us as moms is really the best choice for our kids. And I needed her encouragement.

If that's you right now, don't despair. I know sometimes all the work we put into parenting can seem like it's not making a difference. Or even if we know it is making a difference, we might feel drained by the effort. Just know today—right now—that all the effort you are putting into being a mom matters. It counts. It is impacting your kids. *It is worth it.*

And if you know a mom who might be feeling

discouraged or tired, or who might just need a few kind words like I did that day in Starbucks, be the one to reach out and lift her up. Tell her she's a good mom. Send her a card, text or call her, or even bring her flowers or a meal. A little encouragement really can go a long way.

> **Be More Blissful:** Take a minute to think of a mom in your life and go call her or send her a text, with the sole purpose of lifting her up and sharing some encouraging words or a compliment. You will make her day, and you never know . . . you might be the one who is meant to give her the words she needs to hear right now.

A few years ago, when the kids and I had some time in the car, I decided it would be good to review some safety rules with them. It had been a while since we'd done this and I wanted to review what to do in different types of emergency situations.

I started talking about the importance of sticking together in crowded places like the movie theater or the mall, when Katie chimed in from the back seat . . .

"Yeah, because if we are just one, we can really break. And if we're together, it's not so easy."

I was instantly struck by the wisdom in her words. I asked her where she learned that and she said it was at church when they were going over the verse in Ecclesiastes:

"Though one may be overpowered,
two can defend themselves.
A cord of three strands is not quickly broken."
—*Ecclesiastes 4:12 NIV*

And it's so true—whether in safety situations, life in general, or in motherhood. When we reach out to each other as moms, we don't break as easily. We can defend ourselves against discouragement and weariness. If one of us faces hardship, the other can help us through it. If one can't take another step alone, the other can hold our hand and pull us forward. If one gets discouraged, the other can help us cheer up, or smile, or even laugh.

It can be easy to get busy and forget how important connection with other moms is. But we were meant to reach out to each other and support each other. We weren't meant to be "just one." I hope as you read these words you are reminded that you aren't alone in your parenting journey, that there are many moms out there who are feeling the way you are feeling right now, and going through what you are going through. Sometimes we just need to take that step to reach out to find that connection.

Not long ago, in that same coffee shop where I do a lot of writing, I'd just gotten my coffee and sat down to get some work done when a woman walked over and set a vase of flowers down on the table next to me. She dug in her purse, pulled out an envelope, and leaned it against the vase, *just so*. Then she settled in her chair and checked her watch. Every few minutes, she looked out the window, obviously waiting for someone. I smiled, knowing that whoever was meeting her was going to get a beautiful surprise when they got there.

About five minutes later, another woman walked in. She headed toward the table where her friend was waiting. When she saw the flowers, she stopped. "You are *so* sweet!" she said. "Those are *gorgeous!*"

"Happy Birthday!" her friend laughed, getting up and hugging her. I sipped my coffee, pretended to be writing, and tried not to cry (because the whole scene choked me up).

"You didn't have to *do* that," the friend said.

"I wanted to. It's your *birthday*," said the other. They went to the counter and got their coffees, then sat down at the table and started talking. And it reminded me that even something as simple as a birthday coffee date, a quick walk together, a park play date (where the kids can play so you can talk), or even a card or phone call, can keep us connected with others.

> **Be More Blissful:** If you are someone who has a hard time making that connection with others or finding time to make plans, choose one of your friend's birthdays as an excuse to get together. Sometimes, having a reason makes it easier to get it on the calendar and make it happen!

Reaching out not only means encouraging other moms and getting together, it also means involving our kids in touching the lives of others. When I think about this, I think about the man named Ted who lives in a senior living home near our house. I only met him once, but he's had a place in my heart ever since.

I first saw Ted several years ago, when I was out running errands. I'd been driving by the home and noticed him sitting out front, watching cars go by. As I drove past, I wondered what he was doing. *Was he waiting for a ride? Was someone coming to visit him?* He stayed on my mind for a while.

A couple days later, I was on the same road, at about the same time, and there he was again—white haired, tall and thin. And all by himself. Again, I wondered . . . *Did he have family? Friends? Was he lonely?*

I thought about him the whole way home.

When I saw him *again* a few days later, I felt a pull to stop and talk to him—a pull so strong that I slowed down and turned into a parking lot nearby, thinking I should go back. But when I looked at the time, I realized I only had fifteen minutes to pick Luke up from school. I sighed and drove off, promising that next time I'd stop and say hi.

And as I drove, I realized, I didn't have to wait until next time.

"Want to surprise someone today?" I asked Luke when I picked him up. I told him about my idea and the man I'd seen. We went home and cut roses from our yard. I took the thorns off, and we made a bouquet. Then we drove back to the home. But when we got there, the man was gone. I parked the car and we went inside, hoping to find him.

"Can I help you?" the woman at the front office asked as we walked in.

"This might sound strange," I started nervously, "but I'm looking for a man who sits outside in the mornings, right out front. He's tall and has white hair—"

"That sounds like Ted," she said, smiling.

I showed her the roses. "We wanted to give him these."

"He was *just* here," she said, looking around the lobby. "Oh! There he is," she said, pointing by the stairs. Luke and I walked up to him.

"Ted?" I asked. He nodded. I introduced myself. "I see you in the mornings sometimes when I drive by." I held out the bouquet. "We just wanted to give you these and say hi."

Slowly, he took the roses, a look of surprise on his face. "Thank you," he whispered. Then he turned to Luke and reached out his hand. (It's beautiful to see the hand of a child wrapped inside that of a ninety-or-so-year-old man.) He asked Luke what his name was, and he thanked us again. We only stayed for a minute before saying goodbye. But in that moment, Ted made his way into our hearts, forever.

When Mike and I took the kids to the same home that Christmas to deliver some cards that they'd made, they walked up and down the halls looking for a door with the name Ted on it. When they found one, they picked out their favorite card and set it on the floor in front of the door. And to this day, when I drive down that road, I look for Ted sitting outside.

The best part is so do Katie and Luke.

Mom-to-Mom: When was the last time you went out of your way to reach out to others? Find one way you can involve your kids in reaching out to others this week. What are some ways you can go out of your way to love those closest to you (your husband, your kids, your family)?

Heart-to-Heart: "This is how we know what love is: Jesus Christ laid down his life for us. And we ought to lay down our lives for our brothers and sisters."
—1 John 3:16 NIV

Can you think of a time someone went out of their way for you? What happened as a result? How did it impact you?

A Mom's Prayer: *God, please help me remember that there are people all around me that need love and encouragement. On the days I feel drained or tired and have nothing left to give, fill me with your love and put people in my path who You want me to reach out to. The next time I feel a nudge to do something for someone else, help me to do it. And help me to involve my kids in the process too. I want to teach them to love like You do. Amen.*

Tip #12

Love Your Strengths
(And don't be so hard on yourself.)

"We are more fearful of our weaknesses than
we are honoring of our strengths."
—Marcus Buckingham, from WOF conference

As moms, we're pretty good at knowing what our weaknesses are, aren't we? If someone asks us what areas we want to improve in, we're probably quick to answer. We'd like to be more confident. More organized. More disciplined. More *superwomanish.* The list could go on and on.

But what about our strengths?

Sometimes we get so focused on our weaknesses and comparing ourselves to others that we forget about our own gifts and talents. But knowing and appreciating our strengths can play a key role in finding mommy bliss. If I'm not a crafty mom, but I spend too much time *trying* to be crafty—taking scrapbook classes and browsing the internet to learn how to come up with the perfect project—will I end up joyful or drained? Drained, because that's not my strength (been there, done that!). I admire my friends who can create gorgeous scrapbooks or come up with art projects, but that's not me. Give me Pinterest and a whole bunch of samples, but don't make me come up with my own ideas! And you know what? That's not a weakness, although I used to think it was.

I used to think I needed to improve in this area even though inside, I don't enjoy crafts.

As moms, we need to spend less time wishing we were more like others and just *be ourselves*, because we are the exact moms our kids need. And you know what? It's exciting when you look at parenting that way: that you're a mom gifted with specific strengths and you can use those strengths in unique and effective ways to raise your kids. All moms were not meant to be equal and that is okay.

A while ago, I got an invitation that really made me stop and think about my strengths and the things I was spending my time on. The invitation was to join a group of writers and artists that meet in San Francisco once a week, which is about an hour and a half from my house. The woman who invited me wrote something like . . .

I enjoyed looking through your website and blog, as well as some of your articles. Very interesting background and set of areas you work in—you sure keep yourself busy!

Her invitation was sweet and I was honored to be included, but for some reason her comment really struck me. I wanted to join the group, but driving mid-week to San Francisco at night wasn't really an option with all I had on my plate at the time, and with the activities Katie and Luke were in. And for some strange reason, her invitation challenged me to stop and consider the pace of my life and what I was involved in.

Because I *was* busy (stressed-out busy, actually). Her comment made me realize I'd said yes to too many things, and I was feeling it. I just hadn't really acknowledged it yet. It wasn't until weeks later, after reading Marcus Buckingham's book, *Find Your Strongest Life* (I'd heard him speak at a Women of Faith conference and bought his book), that I realized why I was feeling pulled in so many directions and why that woman's comment hit a raw point for me.

In the book, Marcus urges women to unbalance their lives toward their strengths, rather than constantly struggling for balance in all areas (isn't that what we do so often?). Instead of keeping different areas of life separate from each other, he suggests letting the walls down and leaning into what you are strong at.

When I heard that concept, I thought about the different roles I had . . . wife, mom, children's book author, parenting blogger/writer, volunteer at a non-profit called Courage Worldwide that helps trafficking victims, leader of a hospitality team at church, book reviewer, Assistant Regional Advisor for SCBWI, part-time employee at a publishing company . . . and that wasn't all. I was definitely wearing a lot of hats and I kept many of them on separate shelves as I tried to balance everything. And even though I was passionate about many of the things I was doing, there were just too many things.

And you know what I realized? Some of them were not even in my area of strengths; they left me feeling drained. Somehow, I had gotten into a pattern of saying yes to pretty much every need that crossed my path, and I suddenly wanted more than anything to take down the walls in my life, eliminate the compartments, and focus on the moments that would fill my one cup, as Marcus says. It was a refreshing way to look at things.

> **Be More Blissful: Write a list of all the things you are involved in right now and all of your commitments. Take time to review your list and identify activities you are doing that you dread, or that stress you out. Then identify what changes you might need to make.**

I started to clear some things off my plate. And it was incredibly freeing. I realized that rather than trying to fill every need that comes my way, I could think about whether I was the right person to fill it, whether it fit my individual gifts or would only drain me and take time away from my family. As I focused more on the areas I felt called toward and applied my strengths in those areas, my life changed.

I was still busy, but it became an I-can't-wait-to-get-up-the-next-day-and-do-it-again kind of busy. When we "uncompartmentalize" our lives as moms, intentionally breaking down the walls and removing the separate shelves like Marcus suggests, we are able to celebrate our strengths more (instead of trying to be everything to everybody), and we feel lighter and more empowered to be the woman God created us to be. We spend less time trying to measure up to the expectations of others in projects we aren't passionate about, we aren't spread too thin on this committee or that, we have more time to focus on our families and ourselves, and we can explore and use our talents in new and exciting ways.

And that leaves us feeling *way* more blissful.

Sometimes loving your strengths is also about giving yourself permission to take that next step toward the thing that is tugging at your heart. Even if you aren't sure if you are qualified or ready. Sometimes, it is following that type of tugging that can impact your life, and your joy, the most.

Years ago, about six months after Katie was born, I sat in church one day listening to a guest speaker talk about the need in my community for mentors for teen moms. I instantly felt a tug on my heart. Being a new mom myself, I knew how challenging taking care of a baby could be. I tried to imagine what it would be like to be a teenager with a newborn, and it choked me up. I couldn't deny the pull I felt to get involved.

But, quickly, doubt set in . . .

Me? I thought. *A mentor to teen moms? Who am I to help other moms when I'm just learning how to be a mom myself?*

I brought a brochure that the guest speaker had handed out home and read more about the Mentor Mom program through Youth for Christ. But I didn't call. Instead, I listened to that voice of doubt that said I wasn't good enough, or ready enough . . . and I talked myself out of responding to the tug on my heart.

But even though I didn't take action right away, the pull I felt wouldn't leave. I remember looking at Katie asleep in her bassinet and marveling at her—her tiny hands, her rosy cheeks, her little feet. And then I would think about the teen moms who might be looking at their babies too, and I wondered how they felt about being a mom.

When Mike was out of town (he travelled a lot during that time), and I would be up in the middle of the night with Katie crying, I sometimes felt alone and exhausted. And I would think about how alone those teen moms might be feeling.

I was confused by the pull I felt to get involved and help. It didn't make sense to me—this tug to mentor young moms. I felt totally inadequate, and truthfully, the thought of being a mentor scared me. But I couldn't deny what was happening in my heart. Have you ever felt that way?

Against all logic, and unsure how it would turn out, I finally ended up pushing aside the doubt and I called the Mentor Mom program, went through their training, and got involved in their mentor program. I was scared and unsure, but God knew more than I did that He had given me a passion to encourage other moms. A passion and strength I didn't even know I had yet.

Over the next several years in that program, I had the privilege of coming alongside teen moms—moms with different stories, different backgrounds, and different challenges—and mentoring them. I didn't have parenting all figured out (I still don't!), and I didn't have a lot of experience. But I quickly learned that wasn't what it was all about. It was about saying yes and using my gifts to be there for a teen mom during a hard time. It was about letting her know she wasn't alone in her frustrations and questions. It was about supporting her as she learned, and it was about helping her understand how much God loves her.

Sometimes, I think we don't fully discover our strengths because we let doubt or fear keep us from moving forward. When we feel a tug on our hearts, when we have a burning passion inside, even if we don't understand it, it is there for a reason. Yet so often, we minimize these feelings, put things off for later, or hold back because we doubt what we are feeling or our own abilities. When we do that, we miss an opportunity to make a difference. We miss a chance to see how God can take that small seed of desire (that He planted in our hearts to begin with) and grow it. But when we say yes—even if we aren't sure if we're qualified or how it's all going to turn out—that's when He opens new doors to discover, live, and love our strengths. And by the way, that's when lives are changed, including ours.

And that's when, one by one, the world is changed too.

Mom-to-Mom: What is one thing or activity you feel you are good at? What about something you don't feel you are good at? What is one thing you want to be doing more of right now? What about less of?

Heart-to-Heart: "Every good and perfect gift is from above, coming down from the father of heavenly lights, who does not change like shifting shadows."
—*James 1:17 NIV*

Do you consider your strengths gifts? Do you find yourself dwelling on your weaknesses? What is one way you can appreciate your own strengths more?

A Mom's Prayer: *God, thank you for the strengths You have given me. I want to live with passion and energy, not waste time on things You never intended me to be doing. Keep my focus on what You want me to do and help me identify and appreciate my strengths, and the strengths of my kids more. Amen.*

Tip #13

Love Your Dreams
(You can soar, even when laundry is
blocking your runway!)

"You are never too old to set another goal or to dream a new dream."—C. S. Lewis

Do you remember the hopes and dreams you had for your life . . . but barely? How many of us, after becoming moms, lose sight of the passion that once stirred our hearts? How many of us have stopped *dreaming new dreams?* I know, I know. There are mouths to feed, rooms to clean, and dishes to wash. Who has time to dream? Sometimes it's hard to soar when you have piles of laundry blocking your runway!

But even though being a mom means you have more on your plate for sure, it shouldn't mean setting your dreams on a shelf forever. Yet sometimes that does happen. With the pace and schedule that comes with motherhood, it can be easy to slip into the mode of putting everyone's needs ahead of our own, and forget about our dreams in the process.

Maybe you're feeling like that right now: that you have all these dreams for the people in your life—your kids and your husband and your family—but maybe you've forgotten your own. Or maybe you've put them on the shelf and are wondering if you'll ever get them back down.

We all know that having a dream—having something we're passionate about—is important. But sometimes it can be hard to make that passion a priority. Just because we grow up and have kids doesn't mean we should stop wondering about the possibilities in life, or about the possibilities in ourselves. It doesn't mean we should get stuck in a rut or put limits around everything we once hoped for either.

In the movie *The Adventures of Sharkboy and Lavagirl,* the teacher tells his student Max to stop dreaming. "Dreaming keeps you from seeing what's right here in front of you," he says. But, honestly, I think that's the point. Sometimes we *need* to look past what's in front of us so we can see where we're supposed to go.

Luke has helped me remember this from time to time with his imaginative ideas and outside-the-box thinking. When he was younger and lost his first tooth, he wrote this note to the tooth fairy:

> *dear tooth fary,*
> *can you pleas give me super powrs, fors shealds,*
> *and flying powrs?*
> *and rembr, you don't have to, but pleas do!!!!!!!*

From his young perspective, why bother getting money for a tooth when you can ask for force shields and super powers? I love it (don't you?), but I have to admit, when I first read his note, I tried to do the "motherly" thing and prepare him for reality: that the tooth fairy might not really be able to grant him super powers. I didn't want him to be disappointed when he woke up in the morning.

"But Mom," he said. "She *might*. So I'm gonna ask her." I loved his *why not* perspective. And he reminded me: isn't that how cars and airplanes and spaceships came about? First, someone had a dream that it was possible?

Maybe your dream *is* to be a mom. I can relate; that's definitely always been one of my dreams. Ever since I was a little girl, I knew I wanted to have kids. And you know what? Sometimes, becoming a mom is the very thing that can give our dreams wings.

Be More Blissful: Stop and think about what's stopping you. Are you waiting to pursue your dreams? Have you forgotten what your dreams are or what your passions were before kids? Write down what might be keeping you from moving forward. Then hold that thought. We'll come back to this in a minute.

I remember the day I decided to pursue my dream of being a writer. I sat there at a conference listening to one of the speakers. She shared a story about a woman who came up to her and said she wished she could be a writer like she was. When I heard that, my heart stirred. Because I wanted to be a writer, too. When I was little, I entered my poems in poetry contests. In elementary school, I wrote stories that got published in an anthology my school district printed. And in high school, my favorite classes were about literature and writing.

So how was it that years later, sitting at that conference, I found myself so far away from what I loved? After getting my MBA, working at HP for several years, and then making the decision to be a stay-at-home mom (a decision I've never regretted), I felt a new tug on my heart. The distance from the corporate world and the time I was able to spend reading children's books to my kids had reawakened my passion for writing. I dreamed of writing a book—I wanted to make a difference in the world—but having been away from writing for so long, my dream seemed far off.

As the speaker talked about the woman who dreamed the same thing, I sat on the edge of my seat, my heart beating fast. And when she shared what she told her, it really hit me. She said something like . . .

Just start. Whether it's five minutes a day, or ten. Just start writing. And then you are a writer.

It was one of the most freeing things I'd ever heard. I didn't have to long to be a writer. Or dream of it. I didn't have to imagine what it would be like or worry that I already missed my chance. All I had to do was start. And so I did. In between diaper changes and potty training and play dates, in between preschool and doctor appointments and swim lessons, I researched and read, and started to write. Sometimes I wrote ten minutes a day because that's all I had. Sometimes, on days when the kids took long naps, I wrote more.

It wasn't easy. But nothing worthwhile is. And years later, after many rejection letters, and after signing my first book contracts, I was more thankful than ever that I started. So if you're in the same place I was—wishing for your dream to come true, but not sure how to make it happen . . . just start.

> **Be More Blissful: Here are some tips to help you get started:**
>
> **TIP #1: Just start.** You don't have to wait for the perfect time to pursue your dreams. If something is tugging at your heart and you long to do it, *begin.* God put those desires in your heart for a reason. And don't worry about taking a big leap all at once. Sometimes baby steps are all you have time for when you have kids, and that's okay!
>
> **TIP #2: Expect challenges and don't face them alone,** because sometimes pursuing dreams isn't easy. Come alongside others and share your dreams. You never know what doors will open as a result. Dreaming with someone else is better than dreaming alone!
>
> **TIP #3: Be willing to shift gears.** If you keep hitting your head up against a wall, consider changing direction, but not abandoning your dreams. Maybe all you need are a few minor tweaks. Sometimes, when we think we are

getting a no to our dreams (like the rejection letters I got on some of my manuscripts), we are really getting more time or more training that we might need to succeed. Not every setback is a no!

TIP #4: Be willing to make mistakes. Don't hold off on doing something because you are waiting for the perfect plan. Sometimes, our mistakes can bring the biggest blessings. And, by the way, there is no perfect.

If starting to pursue your dreams sounds scary or intimidating, you are not alone. Sometimes we hold back or don't go after our dreams because of fear or lack of confidence. It's hard enough knowing if we are doing the right thing with our kids, but to also try to figure out the passions of our hearts and why God created us? When we start to think big like that, it's not uncommon for feelings of doubt and inadequacy to set in quickly (after all, we have an enemy who wants to keep us from soaring!). You might be thinking about that dream you always wanted to pursue—starting your own business? Writing that book? Getting that degree?—but maybe you are struggling with uncertainty. Maybe the voice of doubt has set in and you are wondering, *Am I capable? Could I really accomplish it? Do I have what it takes?* It can be easy to listen to that voice of doubt and hold back, wait, and put off pursuing your dreams.

But don't! The doubts are lies, and you are capable. Feelings of fear, especially if you are stepping out into new, unknown territory, are normal. If you're feeling less than confident today—if you doubt your dreams or your abilities—take a minute to remember God put those dreams in your heart for a reason. Take a minute to pray this verse and *believe* . . .

"I can do all things through Christ
who strengthens me."
—*Philippians 4:13*

Does believing you can achieve your dream mean you'll never feel insecure while trying? No. We all go through periods where we question our abilities, depending on what we're facing. But we can trust that when that happens, we can turn to the unshakeable foundation of God's love for strength and confidence. And that's a confidence that can carry us. So if you're in a place where you feel like you've lost touch with your dreams, where you've forgotten what you're passionate about, where you find yourself longing to do something with your life but you're not sure what, I encourage you to spend some time thinking about it.

Think back to when you were younger or before you had kids and recall: what did you love doing? What did you used to dream of becoming? The timing of you reading this, and the quickening of your heart as you think about the dreams you've always wanted to pursue, is not a coincidence. God is with you, waiting for you to take that step, and He is more than willing to help you along the way.

> **Be More Blissful:** Back to that dream you were waiting on, the one you've put on a shelf . . . take a deep breath, smile, and get it down! Then pray about it and talk to friends or your husband about it. Sharing your dream is often the first step in moving forward.

Maybe the thing that keeps you from taking the first step in pursuing your dreams, or moving forward is a fear of failure or disappointment. If that's true for you, I want to encourage you not to let that stop you. As a writer, I've had my share of disappointments. The journey of balancing writing into slivers of time between diapers and bottles, preschool and naps, sports and homework, hasn't been easy. Yet, it's been through the trials and failures that I've learned some of the most important lessons in my journey.

I'll never forget the time I got a two-page rejection letter on my middle grade novel when I first sent it to a publisher. I answered the door, was handed a FedEx envelope, and immediately saw that it had come from the publisher I'd sent my manuscript to. I could tell right away it was a rejection. It was thick—the size of my manuscript—and publishers typically don't return manuscripts if they want to offer you a contract. I hurried into our kitchen pantry (the only place I could go and not be interrupted by the kids), opened the envelope with trembling hands, and cried. Tears of frustration. Tears of disappointment. Tears from many years of trying to get a book contract, but not being successful.

I won't lie; it was hard to get that rejection letter. I had been waiting for a year and a half for the editor to get back to me, and based on her interest and initial response, I was hopeful. But once I got past the emotion of the situation (I admit; it took me a few weeks), I realized the letter was like gold—it contained valuable suggestions for revisions from a top editor, and it was those revisions that helped to make the story what it is today. So even though at the time, the letter seemed like a huge setback, it was really a needed part of the process to move me to the next step in my journey.

When we can continue to move toward our dreams, even when we face walls or setbacks, it not only teaches us, it can teach our kids. They can learn how to handle life's disappointments from our example, and it can be a good thing to share our failures and disappointments with our kids. I'm not saying we should burden them with any bad news we get or tell them things before they are ready or old enough, but sharing challenges we've faced or are facing gives them a chance to see how we handle it. And it equips them with a concrete example of how to handle disappointments in their own lives too.

Sure, I wouldn't have minded getting a book contract during the first year I started writing. Or the second year, or the third . . . you get the point. But, I have to say, standing where I am today and looking back over the whole process, I am honestly grateful for the spurts of failure I experienced in pursuing my dream of becoming an author. Without them, the successes I've had wouldn't be as sweet as they have been.

Without the failure I've known, when my kids face disappointment, like not making a team or not winning a game, I wouldn't be able to say "I know how that feels" and *truly* know how that feels. And I've come to realize that, whatever the dream, the process of getting there can be just as important as the end result. And that, believe it or not, failure actually *can* be sweet when we look at it as an opportunity to learn from—both for us and our kids.

> **Be More Blissful: Talk to your kids about their dreams. Make it a point to encourage them, even at a young age, to think about what they like to do and what they imagine themselves doing when they grow up. Remind them that all things are possible (Philippians 4:13) and help them understand the positive impact they can have on the world.**

Maybe fear of failure isn't an issue for you at all. Maybe you've simply put your dreams aside because you are at a stage where things are too crazy with babies and toddlers to imagine what else you'd want to do with your life if you had an extra minute. If that's you, it's okay. Before you know it, the time will come when you *will* have a minute. Sometimes, depending on our kids' ages and the season that we are in, we do need to put our dreams on a shelf for a while. Just make sure you don't leave them there and forget about them. Rest in knowing that you are doing something important and mighty right now, just by being a mom. Your other dreams will be ready for you when you are ready to pursue them. And a last note about dreams, mom. Our dreams aren't just about us and our passions or desires. When our kids see us dreaming, they learn to dream too.

Mom-to-Mom: Are you pursuing your dreams right now? Why or why not? What is one thing you like or are passionate about that you have put on a shelf since becoming a mom?

Heart-to-Heart: "But those who hope in the LORD will renew their strength. They will soar on wings like eagles; they will run and not grow weary, they will walk and not be faint."
  —*Isaiah 40:31 NIV*

Do you feel like you're soaring when it comes to pursuing your passions? Or are you weary and faint? Have you asked God about your dreams? He created you and knows the plan for your life; put your hope in Him and He *will* help you soar.

A Mom's Prayer: *God, I lay my dreams at your feet. If I've lost touch with something You created me to do, please* *revive that passion and stir my heart. If I'm pursuing some-thing that doesn't fit into Your plan for me, please help me to let go of it and accept closed doors. Please give me wisdom and patience as You lead me on Your path, according to Your timeline. Please help me pursue my dreams; I want to soar! Amen.*

Tip #14

Take Time
(Or it will take you.)

"Work is not always required.
There is such a thing as sacred idleness."—George
MacDonald

You slink away to your bathroom, close the door and lock it. You've told your husband that you are taking a bath. You've told the kids, too, and asked them to go to Daddy if they need anything. You've made sure everyone is fed and homework is done and you've explained that mommy needs a little time to herself. *There are to be no interruptions.* You're as clear as you can be. Behind the closed door, you let out a sigh.

You fill the tub with hot water and take a deep breath, savoring the moment. You slide down into the bubbles. Within two minutes—no, maybe one—there's a knock on the door. "Mommy?"

You groan. "What?"

"Can I come in too?"

"No," you tell your daughter. "Remember what I said? Go play and I'll be out in a bit." You sigh again and close your eyes.

"But, Mommy? What are you doing in there?"

"I'm taking a bath. Now go play, okay?" Your voice gets a little louder.

Little footsteps disappear down the hall. *Finally*, you

think. But five minutes later, just as you are starting to fully relax, there's another knock. "Mommy?" It's your son this time.

"What?" There's an edge to your voice.

"Can you help me find my yo-yo?"

"No. I'm in the bath. Go ask Daddy."

"He's busy."

"Well so am I!" (Maybe a little bit too much of an edge.) You soften it a bit . . . "I'll be out soon. We'll look for your yo-yo then."

"But then what am I supposed to play?"

You clench your jaw. Slowly . . . "You can play whatever you want. Go ask Daddy to play with you."

Three minutes pass. You're watching the clock. You exhale, listening intently for more footsteps. You wait. But when you don't hear any, you smile and picture the kids finally occupied. You sink lower into the bubbles.

There's another knock. "Hon?" It's your husband this time.

"What?"

"How much longer are you going to be?"

And that's when you know you should've gone to a spa or somewhere—anywhere—*away from home* so you could really get a little time alone.

I'm sure you've had a situation similar to this one, probably even within the last week. In fact, finding a slice of time to ourselves may be one of the hardest areas for us moms to conquer. I've been guilty of not setting aside time for myself for sure. There have been times when I've gotten gift certificates for massages that I've held onto for almost a year, simply because I didn't take the time. But that's not good for us. Or our families.

My friend Laura Faudree, who is a MFT and Director of the Soul Care Center at Bridgeway Christian Church in California, says, "If moms make time for themselves, everyone is happier. We parent better, get less angry, and have more fun with our kids. This is a belief I think we all believe in theory, but not many of us put it into actions. It is healthy to want, need, and take *me* time."

As moms, we want to raise confident kids who grow into adults that love and respect themselves. But in order to do this, we need to appreciate, love, and respect ourselves first. This can be especially hard because as moms, we tend to take care of everyone else's needs before our own.

A while ago, I found out I was low on vitamin D, so I decided I needed to get more sunshine. I decided I'd spend ten minutes a day outside. It actually sounded *wonderful*. But I had no idea it was going to be such a challenge to make the time—a small slice of time—for myself. When the sun was out, I'd look out the window and think, *It is perfect out there. I need to get outside. And I will . . . in a minute.* Then I'd finish e-mails, fold the laundry, make a few phone calls, get some writing done, pay the bills . . . and the next thing I knew, it was time to pick the kids up from school, help them with their homework, run off to basketball or piano, and figure out dinner.

Or (and this was even worse) when I *did* get outside, I'd have a hard time shaking the feeling that I shouldn't be *just sitting there*. It was challenging to turn the to-do list off in my head. Yet on the days I was able to get outside and sit—*just sit*—in the sunshine, it truly made a difference in my mood. That little slice of time to myself was heaven. And when I went back inside, I was relaxed, warm, and content. All from ten little minutes of being still.

> **Be More Blissful: Stop reading and go spend ten minutes outside right now. I'm serious. (Don't listen to that voice in your head telling you to skip this part! It really will make a difference). If it's too cold or if the weather is miserable, find a cozy, relaxing spot in your house and just be still. You deserve it, mom.**

A friend of mine had such words of wisdom about this. We were helping at our kids' school, making copies and chatting, when she shared with me that every day she takes one hour to herself, "Because our jobs are 24/7, you know." She takes a break and does something she enjoys, whether it's have a cup of coffee or watch the news for an hour. "Our jobs are 24/7," she said again. "We never get a break, so we need to take one." And she's right. If we *don't* take time to refuel as moms, our parenting will show it.

If we want to be healthy and happy moms, we need to take the *time* to be healthy and happy moms. We need to choose to take time for ourselves, to exercise, eat right, decompress, pray, and do other things that are emotionally fulfilling and physically recharging. If we don't, we risk ending up high-strung, stressed out, not feeling good about ourselves, and even resentful towards the people in our lives we love the most. But when we do take the time—even if it's just ten minutes or a half hour—we are able to put our priorities into focus and pause and appreciate things more.

Taking time for yourself matters on the bliss scale, mom. Give yourself permission to have a mommy time out when you need it, and promise me you won't feel guilty about it.

> **Be More Blissful:** Find some time for fun this week! Think about an activity you enjoy, then go do it! Invite other moms and be the one to pave the way for taking time to refresh.

In addition to taking time for ourselves, it's also important to take time with our kids. We've already talked about the importance of slowing down, but the more intentional we are about setting aside time with our kids and paying attention to the quality of the time we spend with them, the more positive our impact can be. And the more blissful our time together.

While the quality of our own time alone is often determined by the peace and quiet we experience, the time we spend with our kids is often defined by what we say and how we say it. Especially as our kids get older and hit the pre-teen and teenage years, communication can become more of a challenge. As they naturally start to separate from us, it can be more difficult to find a connection with them through conversation. Silent car rides and dinner talk that consists of one word answers may even become the norm for a little while. And it's especially then that our words and the way we say them become even more important.

I'm sure you remember things your mom said that encouraged you in some way and made a big difference, or things that still hurt when you think about them. And we've all said something to our own kids that we've regretted at one time or another. Words have the power to define whether time spent with our kids is quality time, or not. If we set aside time with our kids, but say things that negatively impact them, or spend time arguing, nobody is going to feel healthier or happier.

> **Be More Blissful:** When you spend time with your kids this week, try to be aware of what you are saying and how you say it. Why not make it a point to say something like: 1. "It's okay. I've made mistakes too." 2. "I don't know the answer, but we can look into that together." 3. "You can do it. I believe in you."

As Katie and Luke hit their pre-teen and teen years, we started to experience less communication in our own house. I talked to a friend about what we were seeing and she suggested we use table questions to spur conversation. You can find table-talk questions in different formats online. So I did some digging, put together some questions, and we began using what I called Heikka Family Table Talk cards at dinner. To this day, we keep a small basket on our kitchen counter filled with pieces of paper that have questions on them. Some of the questions are broad, like, "If you could do one thing to change the world, what would it be and why?" and some are specific like, "What was one good thing that happened to you today?" When we sit down as a family to eat, I grab the basket and casually start asking some questions. The kids join in and ask Mike and me questions too, and the cards help bring fun and interesting conversation into our mealtime.

I know taking time for yourself, or making the best of the time you spend with your kids isn't always easy, but it's worth it. Even if your kids miss you terribly when you're able to peel yourself away for a bath or time with friends, or even if they are older and seem less-than-thrilled to have you talking to them when you are together, you will feel happier and they will learn from your example when you make the effort.

Mom-to-Mom: How do you set aside time for yourself, or do you struggle in this area? What about spending time with your kids? What are the things that you do that leave you—and your kids—feeling happier, and healthier?

Heart-to-Heart: "Then Jesus went with his disciples to a place called Gethsemane, and he said to them, 'Sit here while I go over there and pray.'"
—*Matthew 26:36 NIV*

Even Jesus took time alone. In those times, he prayed and drew close to God. When was the last time you did that? What was the result?

A Mom's Prayer: *I so needed this today, God. Thank you. It's reassuring to know that even You took time away. Sometimes things get so busy that I forget to be still. Please help me to draw close to You before I start each day. Help me to take time to listen to Your voice, and help me to start setting aside time for myself so I can be the best mom I can be. Help me also to take time with my kids and have clear communication with them. You did not intend for me to rush through each day, feeling stressed or exhausted. Refresh me with your Holy Spirit, and help me quiet my heart by taking time to be still. Amen.*

Tip #15

Cry, For You
(Because you're worth it.)

"Tears are the safety valve of the heart
when too much pressure is laid on it."
—Albert Smith

Moms are experts at *just dealing*. We're pros at delaying stress relief and keeping everything together. But in the same way it's impossible to keep a teapot from eventually whistling to let off steam, we need to find ways to turn down the heat and get relief from the pressure too.

Crying can help; it not only releases toxins, it also releases stress hormones. If we don't let our stress out, it can literally affect our health—physical *and* emotional. Charles Dickens writes in his book *Oliver Twist* that crying "Opens the lungs, washes the countenance, exercises the eyes, and softens down the temper. So cry away."

Cry away . . .

I can hear you thinking *a whole section dedicated to crying? Who wants to wallow in their tears like that?* But I'm not just talking about the act of crying. Crying isn't only about tears. It's also about strength, healing, and acknowledging your feelings. We all have a story, and if I had to guess, I'd say we all have at least one thing from our past—maybe big, maybe little—that is affecting our parenting today. At least one thing we might need to seek healing from.

Being a mom can remind you of when you were a child: when your daughter turns eight, you might remember when you were eight too—maybe your third grade teacher or your eighth birthday party. And when your son gets his first pet, you might remember your first pet. The impact from your childhood and what you remember about it as your kids grow up can be positive; maybe your parents had a great marriage and you are following suite. Or maybe you had wonderful family traditions and you are carrying those on with your own family.

But other things from your past might be difficult and might have a negative impact on you, sometimes without you even realizing it. Maybe you're harboring hurt from something someone did to you, or shame from choices you made or something you did. Maybe some memories you have from your childhood are not so good, and over the years you've stuffed them away and tried to ignore them.

But the problem with that is those feelings don't disappear on their own; instead, they often show themselves in other ways. Sometimes, in your parenting. Unresolved feelings and emotions from your past can have a huge impact on your joy today, mom. Have you stuffed a painful memory inside, and it's coming out as impatience and yelling at your kids? Do you distance yourself from your husband because you are struggling with how you feel about yourself? Do you have fear that your kids will be hurt by others, because you were hurt? Or are you scared they will make poor choices as they grow up, because you did? Are you frustrated with how you respond to certain situations, but you don't know how to parent any other way? Maybe you have unresolved hurt, disappointment, shame, or pain that you're carrying around in your journey as a mom.

Finding mommy bliss is so much about loving the mom that you are. But what if your past hurts or regrets leave you feeling like you don't love yourself? What then?

That's where the "crying" comes in—the letting yourself feel those emotions, then working through those feelings. "Struggling with the past can prevent you from experiencing joy as a mom in the present," says my friend Laura Faudree. "We all have baggage, negative experiences or painful memories that sometimes shape how we deal with the world around us. The misconception is that we think what we have done or what has happened to us has made us who we are. If you think you are a product of all the negative things that have happened to you, if you let those negative experiences define you, then you tend to walk around in bondage instead of freedom. When you are able to separate who you are from what has happened to you, you are more stable and able to use your internal resources to overcome anything that comes your way," says Laura.

Don't let hurt or shame be your identity, mom. And don't skip over this section because it's uncomfortable or because it sounds like it might be too much work. Avoiding your feelings won't bring you freedom, or bliss (I've been there). If you truly want to experience all the joy that God has for you as a mom, I encourage you to let go of the baggage you've been carrying, whether it's a tiny purse or a huge suitcase. After all, the size doesn't always determine the weight.

As moms, we will have a variety of emotions on our parenting journey. I love how Laura reminds us, "Most of the time what trips us up is our feelings about our feelings. Having a range of emotions is normal and natural. Our children bring us the greatest joy imaginable, and sometimes the worst pain. Don't beat yourself up over the emotions. Acknowledge, accept, grieve if you need to, and then you are much more able to move on."

Be More Blissful: Pause for a minute and consider: Have you acknowledged? Accepted? Grieved?

By taking the time to work through past issues or feelings that might be weighing us down, whether those feelings might be anger, regret, fear, shame, guilt, or something else, we are able to find our way out of it and move on. We are able to drop the baggage so we don't carry it around in our daily roles as moms. Actively pursuing healing (crying for you) is a key to finding mommy bliss. Let me say that again, mom. *Actively pursuing healing from the things that might be holding you back (crying for you) is a key to finding mommy bliss.* And even though that might sound scary, complicated, or like too much work, crying for you doesn't mean you have to dwell there.

Sometimes we simply need to look to the past before we can be free to enjoy the present, and the future. And we need to be free, mom. Because our freedom directly impacts the freedom of our kids.

Be More Blissful: Take a minute to be honest with yourself: Are you totally free, or are there hurts and burdens you're carrying that are weighing you (and your parenting) down? Write one thing down that you want to be free from. Naming it can be the first step in acknowledging how you feel and moving toward freedom. Then take the time to pursue any healing you might need. Digging into the past can be hard, but the joy on the other side is worth it. Sometimes the first step in this process is simply praying for courage.

For years, I minimized a few things I had tucked away, telling myself they weren't a big deal and they didn't really matter. But here's the thing: unresolved hurts always come out in some way. And for me, they manifested as a struggle with self-worth and food in college. During those years, I lived in a secret world of rituals, routines, and rules, yet nobody really knew the extent of it.

Even after I started to pull out of it (understanding God's love for me for the first time was the starting point of my healing), I didn't talk about my struggle. It wasn't until years later when I started to write a fictional novel about a teenager with an eating disorder that was loosely based on my own experiences that I opened up and shared with Mike, my family, and some friends what I had gone through. The writing—taking time to *go there*—was cathartic for me; I spent hours typing through tears as I recalled the memories of that dark time in my life. As I *cried for me.* But you know what I found? There was healing on the other side—in sharing what I went through with others, even the embarrassing parts or the stuff I had kept hidden.

Healing is sometimes like peeling back the layers of an onion, and it can take a long time. Though I had found healing from my struggle with food, it wasn't until years later, after Mike and I got married, had the kids, and Katie and Luke approached their pre-teen years that I unexpectedly sensed another layer needing to be peeled back. Watching them grow up made me reflect on myself and my own journey growing up. There was a lot of good that I was excited to pass onto them. But, to be honest, I started to have some fear as a mom about the teenage years. I didn't want them to face some of the same situations I faced, or make some of the same choices I made.

If you're reading this and your heart is beating fast with the knowing that there is something unresolved you've kept inside for years too—don't wait anymore. I love how Laura encourages women to, "Give yourself permission to acknowledge and accept your feelings because they're real and legitimate. When you do that, you're able to accept your children's ranges of emotions as legitimate too, and you're able to accept them for who they are, and not who you want them to be."

In my own journey of discovering the things that were weighing me down and then finding freedom from them, a key to that freedom was in the telling. (There were things I needed to work through that I didn't even know I needed to work through until I opened up and started talking about them!) Finding even one trusted person to share your feelings with can make a difference. Hurts, regrets, or difficult memories are magnified when they're stuffed down and kept in secret. They can hold you back from being the woman and mom you were meant to be. But when they're brought out into the open—no matter how big, small, horrible, embarrassing, or stupid you think they might be—they somehow lose that power.

My friend Barbara Wilson, who is the author of several books on healing for women, recommends finding a counselor or safe person to talk to about the things that are holding you down. "Telling our stories breaks the grip of the secret, diffusing its power. Exposing the secret makes it shrink, while hiding it allows it to grow bigger and uglier. Keeping silent means we bear the load alone. Opening up allows others to share our burden, our pain, our shame. Silence inhibits healing; openness facilitates it. Every time someone shares their secret with me, I can't help becoming excited for them, because I know they are taking the first step towards healing."— From Barbara's book *The Invisible Bond; How to Break Free From Your Sexual Past.*

Spending time reflecting on our past—both the happy and painful memories—gives us a deeper understanding of who we are today. We come to understand why we feel the way we feel, why we do the things we do, what motivates us, what matters most to us, what we are scared of, what we are passionate about, and more—and that's an empowering place to be. I want to encourage you, mom: when we acknowledge and work through our feelings as moms, we become healthier and happier . . . and so do our kids.

If you want to experience all the joy that comes with being a mom, you need to be able let go of any bags you might be carrying around that are filled with burdens. And not pick them up again

Crying for you is not about digging up the past just for the sake of "crying" or feeling sorry for yourself, and it's not about staying there in the past, either. Actually, it's the opposite. It's about being able to move on, let go, and totally heal so you can experience true and lasting joy.

I want you to know that this chapter isn't meant to be all inclusive. In no way do I want to insinuate that all you need to do is reflect on your past, talk to someone about it, and you will be fine. Some things take years to work through, and everyone's healing is different. We all respond uniquely to things we've done or things that have been done to us, and we can't compare our stories or feelings. We also can't expect our paths of healing to be the same. But what we can do is come alongside each other, encourage each other to seek the healing we might need (whether that be therapy, counseling, going through my friend Barbara Wilson's healing Bible study or reading her books, talking to one trusted person, etc.), and support each other.

I encourage you to think about whether you are truly free, mom. Or whether you need to cry, for you. When we intentionally set out to cry for ourselves, when we are willing to trust the journey of healing even though it can be scary, when we stop stuffing our feelings and pretending like everything is perfect when it's not, true healing can be found.

And true bliss is right there on the other side.

"Forget the former things;
do not dwell on the past.
See, I am doing a new thing!
Now it springs up; do you not perceive it?
I am making a way in the wilderness and
streams in the wasteland."
—*Isaiah 43:18-19 NIV*

Mom-to-Mom: Are there things you've been stuffing, rather than acknowledging? Do you have a hard time crying for yourself? Is there a time you were able to share your burden with others, and felt better?

Heart-to-Heart: "May my cry come before you, Lord; give me understanding according to your word."
—*Psalm 119:169 NIV*

Have you ever let your cry come before the Lord—for healing, for forgiveness, for comfort, for peace? Have you cried for yourself, things you did or others did to you, or past pain and regret? What was the result of doing that?

A Mom's Prayer: *God, You know me inside and out. You know if I need healing and what areas I need healing in. I want to live in the freedom You designed for me, without chains or burdens holding me back. I know You are a God of healing and freedom. Please give me the courage to take whatever steps You are prompting me to take so that I can be free, and healed. Wash over me with Your love and grace. I know the plans You have for me are good. Please help me to trust You fully. Amen.*

Tip # 16

Ask for Help When You Need It
(or: Nobody benefits when you are the martyr, including you.)

"A bend in the road is not the end of the road . . .
unless you fail to make the turn."
—Author Unknown

A couple years ago, I broke my arm and dislocated my knee in two separate, random falls—both within a week of each other. The timing was terrible; Mike was in India for work for ten days and I was alone with the kids.

It was a time of many firsts for me: my first broken bone, my first set of crutches for a torn knee (that I ended up not being able to use because of my broken arm), my first wheelchair (that I ended up getting because I couldn't use the crutches), and my first ride in one of those electric scooters at Target.

I learned a lot, too. Like how to blow dry my hair and put on makeup with my left hand (I had mascara issues!). I also learned how to go up and down the stairs using one arm and one leg and how to type with my cast on.

And—maybe the hardest thing for me—I learned how to accept help from others (because I needed it).

I know what I went through was small compared to what some people have experienced. Tiny, even. But, as someone who usually runs around at full speed and is very independent, it was hard having life come to a sudden halt.

It was also a blessing in disguise. My family and friends stayed with me and helped with dinners, getting the kids to and from activities, and even things like washing my hair. And in spite of my discomfort and pain, we had nice visits, good conversation, and a few good laughs. (Mostly at me—like when I wiped a dot of mustard off my plate with a finger on my right hand, went to lick my finger, and realized I couldn't get it to my mouth because of my cast.)

The experience taught me an important lesson.

Sometimes, as moms, I think we feel like we have to have it all together, and if we need help, we aren't doing our job right. So we hesitate to ask. We don't want people to know we are struggling, or our kids are struggling.

And we just struggle more.

Yet when we ask for and accept help, our load is lightened. Sometimes we don't even realize how beneficial that can be until after the fact.

Be More Blissful: Identify one area you need help in right now, then ask for it. I know it's tempting to gloss over this and continue to do things yourself, but don't. Everyone has something on their plate that they could use help with. You'll be surprised what a difference even talking about your challenges or struggles with someone else will make.

A friend I used to work with—a single mom—was diagnosed with cancer a while ago. She told me that one of the hardest things for her after she started chemo was learning how to ask for help. Even though she was sick, she still felt like she should be able to handle everything on her own. But, she shared that once she got past that and was able to ask for help, it made a huge difference in her healing process.

Stress can impact us in such powerful ways, mom. It can make us feel sick, tired, depressed, anxious, and a million other things. We can even be experiencing symptoms that are being caused by stress, and we don't even know it. I learned that the hard way several years ago, even before my knee and arm episode.

At the time, Mike had been doing a lot of travel for work. Each time he was away, I'd get offers from friends for help. They'd call or stop by and many of them would offer: "If you need anything when Mike's gone, just call."

I'd thank them, but I never even considered taking anyone up on it. It just seemed easier to do things myself, and I wasn't used to asking for help. It has never been a comfortable thing for me. But after a full year of balancing a hectic schedule with young kids and Mike travelling, things came to a head. When he was on one of his business trips—this one to China for about two weeks—I suddenly began to have sleepless nights and migraines.

I had never experienced either before, and it left me frustrated and wondering if I'd ever feel normal again. Those nights of insomnia were hard—alone in the house with the kids sound asleep. I'd lie there for hours trying to get to sleep, thinking about all the things I had to do the next day and all I had on my plate—and the thought of having no sleep to do them created even more sleeplessness. I'd pray and pray, and while that definitely helped, some nights it seemed like morning would never come.

When Mike got home from that particular trip (and I had his help again), my sleepless nights ended. I found out later that I'd been grinding my teeth in my sleep (stress?) and after I got a mouth guard, the headaches ended. I started to feel like myself again.

A few months later, Mike's company put a freeze on travel for a while and he was suddenly home a lot more. It wasn't until that happened that I truly realized how busy the previous year had been. It wasn't until the stress had *lifted* that I realized how stressed I'd actually been.

And isn't that often how it is? We can't see the forest for the trees. Sometimes, when we are stuck in the lap of stress, we don't even know we are there. During that whole year Mike was travelling, in spite of the many offers of help, I had a hard time accepting them.

Why do we do that sometimes? Why do we insist on "doing it all" when we don't have to? Why do we want to keep it all together, or act like we are keeping it all together, so badly? I wonder; if I would've accepted the sweet offers for help from my friends and family that year, would I have experienced the headaches? The sleepless nights? The stress?

We don't have to be sick or suffering from an injury to ask for help. We don't have to be in a crisis, either.

There will be times in our journeys as moms that are harder for us and our families, and there will be times that are easier. We will all go through ups and downs, hills and valleys, and plenty of phases, especially as our kids get older.

We understand the exhaustion, the worry, and the stress that comes with parenting. And we have such power to help each other when things get tough. We take note when another mom is down or struggling, and we try to lift her up. So if we are the one who needs lifting, we should be able to ask for that hand, or accept that shoulder to cry on when it's offered.

That can make for a whole lot *less* stress for a whole lot *more* moms.

And a whole lot more bliss, too.

Mom-to-Mom: Take note of how you're feeling right now, and go back to tip #1 and review the questionnaire you filled out. Do a physical and emotional inventory. Where are you on the bliss scale? Do you feel healthy? Strong? Tired? Depressed? Anxious? In pain? Now ask yourself: Could it have something to do with stress? Would asking for help in some area lighten your load?

Heart-to-Heart: "Therefore encourage one another and build one another up, just as you are doing."
—*1 Thessalonians 5:11 NIV*

Do you need someone to build you up right now? If you could ask for help with one thing, what would it be? Don't worry if it's big or little; the size doesn't always dictate the amount of help you might need.

A Mom's Prayer: *God, I lay my stress at Your feet. I admit; sometimes I feel empty, anxious, or overwhelmed. I have so much to be grateful for, but some days, the minutes run together and everyone needs something from me, and I just feel drained. On those days, please fill me with Your peace. Please help me remember that I don't have to do it all on my own, and I don't have to get it all done today. Please give me the wisdom to ask for help when I need it, and please provide me with a fresh perspective for the areas I'm stressed about right now. Amen.*

Tip #17

Do Your Best
(And God will bless the rest.)

"Failure is simply the opportunity to begin again,
this time more intelligently."—Henry Ford

Do you ever pause and think . . . the *responsibility* of
being a mom? Or the *pressure?* It's a lot to know we are
raising little people to be big people in a big world,
right? It's a lot to think about the fact that our kids are
always watching us and looking up to us, too. We want
to do the right thing *all the time*, but let's face it; sometimes we don't. And beating ourselves up about it can be
a bliss-killer for sure.

While we try to do the best we can, it's important to
remember that sometimes our fumbles as parents can
provide opportunities for teaching—our kids *and* us.
When Katie and Luke were little, we went to Target one
day (well, actually, we went to Target a million days, but
I remember this one particularly well). We were walking down the toy aisle when I saw a Nerf gun Luke had
been wanting. His birthday was around the corner and
I didn't want to have to come back to Target on another
day, so I grabbed the gun and buried it in the cart. I kept
walking, hoping the kids didn't notice.

Not only did Katie see me do it and start digging in
the cart to see what I got, Luke turned and asked what
we were looking at. "Oh, nothing," I said, "Katie just

asked to see something in the cart." I wheeled it away from both of them and pushed it faster down the aisle.

That's when Katie got a look of indignation on her face and stopped walking. "Mommy! You just told a lie!" she shouted. "I didn't *ask* to see *anything* in the cart."

Oops.

Even though I didn't set out to lie, and she *was* digging in the cart to see what I put in there, she was right; she didn't *ask* me. (We moms can't get away with anything!) She didn't miss a beat. But kids are like that; they watch us—how we act, what we say, and if we tell the truth or not. They notice what we listen to on the radio and what we watch on TV. They see how we dress, how we treat people, and how we react to how others treat us. They listen when we pray. And when we don't.

As I said, the *pressure*, right?

I'm the first to admit; I don't always make the right decisions. And, like that day in Target with the Nerf gun, there have been times I've had to apologize and admit my mistakes to my kids.

But here's the important thing: when you mess up, don't beat yourself up. That doesn't do anyone any good. Instead, be honest about your mistakes and learn from them. Then strive to do better or different next time. I know my Target example is pretty lighthearted, but whatever mistakes you've made as a mom, take a minute to forgive yourself. And if there are serious things you are struggling with, be honest with yourself. Are you caught in a behavior that is destructive to you and your kids? Do you struggle with the same mistakes over and over?

If that's the case, reach out to someone for help. Talk to someone about it. Like we talked about in Cry For You, having another person know what you are struggling with and helping you through it can make all the difference.

Taking a look at yourself and your behavior can be hard if you know there are areas you might need to change. But the purpose isn't to make you feel like a bad mom, or feel guilty. In fact, God hates guilt. Christ died to set us *free*, and if there are things we are doing that are holding us in bondage in any way, He waits, full of grace, ready to help us, not condemn us. We just need to be honest with ourselves, others, and Him, determine to make changes, and ask Him for help.

And the good news is, He can redeem our mistakes—big and small. Not only does He forgive us the second we ask for forgiveness, He works all things together for good. Our kids can learn from our good examples *and* our not-so-good ones. And when we are real and admit when we are wrong, they will see that we are human and that sometimes we mess up too.

That kind of humility breeds grace, *and* bliss.

Be More Blissful: Are there things you're doing that you know are setting a bad example for your kids or impacting them negatively? The next time you're tempted to talk bad about someone, tell that white lie, or whatever it might be, consider your audience and take the high road. You'll feel a whole lot better about yourself, and that's a bliss booster for sure.

While it is necessary to look at the bigger changes we might need to make in our own lives, we shouldn't lose sight of the opportunity we have to positively impact our kids through our everyday decisions and actions, too. Sometimes, it's the little things we do and say that can actually make the most impact.

The day after the Fourth of July one year, Mike and I were wavering about going to church. We'd been up late with the kids the night before and we wanted to let them catch up on their sleep. And to be honest, we were tired too. But after going back and forth and feeling a tug that we shouldn't miss, we ended up going.

I was so glad we did.

It turns out that going to church wasn't about us at all. It was about Katie. We had a guest speaker that day that talked about Ephesians 4:8: "Finally, brothers and sisters, whatever is true, whatever is noble, whatever is right, whatever is pure, whatever is lovely, whatever is admirable—if anything is excellent or praiseworthy—think about such things." A few days after we went, Katie came up to me, out of the blue, and said, "Mom, have you noticed that I'm not listening to any of that music lately?" (She'd started wanting to listen to some songs on the radio that weren't exactly—shall we say—positive or uplifting.)

I paused and realized, "I *have*. Did something change?"

She nodded proudly. "It was that verse in church that I heard last weekend. The one that says whatever is good, whatever is pure, whatever is holy." She smiled. "Ever since I heard that verse, I just don't want to listen to it anymore." Katie needed to be at church that weekend, not us. (Well, I'm sure we needed to be there too, but you know what I mean.) And I needed to set the example and get her there. It was a simple decision, but it really impacted her.

As moms, doing an inventory like this—looking closer at the things we say and do and how they influence our kids—can point out both the good and the not-so-good. (While we are talking about making changes to the not-so-good, make sure you also stop and celebrate the good!) It may also reveal things we might not even be aware of. And, believe me, it's always good to check our own attitudes and behaviors (and change them if needed), before our kids show us that we need a little adjusting. I remember a few years ago, during an argument with Katie, she got frustrated with me and said, "Fine! That's just fine, Mom." She folded her arms and did a little *hmph*, and the tone of her voice was the last straw for me.

"We have a new rule around here," I said. "*No* more sarcasm!" I'd had enough. She went on her way, and I went on my way, and after things had settled down, I thought about her tone and wondered, *Where's she getting that from?*

A few days later, I got my answer. And it wasn't the one I wanted. We were finishing breakfast and Katie asked me if she could watch TV before school since she was done getting ready early. We have a rule about no TV before school and I reminded her of that and said no. "You're not fair," she said, and she stomped out of the room moping.

Frustrated, I followed her. "That's great," I said, "You're going to leave for school all upset just because of TV? That's really great."

She turned and looked at me. "Mom," she said softly, "you're being sarcastic. I thought you said we couldn't be sarcastic anymore."

Honestly, it kind of stopped me in my tracks. I didn't even *realize* I was being sarcastic. And it hit me that she was probably getting her sarcasm from me. I apologized and promised to follow the rule, just like her. It was a little bit of a wakeup call for me, and a reminder of just how much my attitude and tone affects my whole family.

> **Be More Blissful:** The next time you wonder, *Where are my kids getting that from?* Ask your-self, *Are they learning it from me?* We have such power as moms to set the tone in our house and for our kids, so let's set it in an uplifting, positive way!

Let me just stop here and say: Don't let all this reminding that your kids are watching you stress you out. Yes, as moms we *should* try to do the right thing and set a good example for our kids all the time (it's good for us too!), but it's not about breaking our backs to try to be perfect. We don't have to "have it all together," all the time. We couldn't even if we tried, right? Being a mom comes with huge responsibility, but rather than putting pressure on ourselves to be perfect, what if we got out of bed each day instead thinking . . . what an *amazing privilege* it is to be able to set an example for another human being on how to live!

And remember, mom; it's about *grace*, too. We give grace to our kids; and we need to give it to ourselves. When Luke was younger and he made his bed on his own, but the covers were all wrinkled and crooked, I didn't tell him that it looked messy; I praised him for getting it done, and my heart smiled at the fact that he tried. When God sees our efforts to follow Him and be the best moms we can be, even if we make mistakes, He smiles at our trying. Life isn't about God measuring us and our efforts; it's about Him loving us.

So take joy in that today, mom. And take a minute to reflect on and celebrate the decisions and sacrifices you've made that have positively impacted your kids. Each day you are growing, each day your heart is expanding, and each day you are blossoming as a mom. Yes, you will make mistakes. But when you put your best foot forward and strive to do your best, God *will* bless the rest.

Mom-to-Mom: What about you? What are some ways you have positively impacted your kids? What about some mistakes you've made or things you might want to improve in? I challenge you to be honest here. Honesty opens the door for change, which often opens the door for bliss.

Heart-to-Heart: "Start children off on the way they should go, and even when they are old they will not turn from it."

—*Proverbs 22:6 NIV*

Are you happy with the example you are setting for your kids? Why or why not? What is one thing you can do differently this week that will more effectively train your children in the way that they should go?

A Mom's Prayer: *God, thank you for forgiving me when I mess up. Help me set a good example for my kids. I know I don't have to be perfect (thank you!), but I ask You to help me be the best mom that I can be. Please guide me and teach me, calling me to a higher path than the one I would set for myself if it were all up to me. Thank you for your grace; I pray that I would have that same grace for myself and my kids. I want them to know how much I love them because of who they are, not because of what they do or don't do. Amen.*

Tip #18

Search the Pieces
(Because bliss is in the bits!)

"A truly happy person is one who can enjoy the scenery while on a detour."—Author Unknown

"I have to tell you the best thing," Katie said to me one night, smiling. She'd just gotten home from youth group and finished brushing her teeth and putting her pajamas on. I sat down on the edge of her bed.

"You know how happiness doesn't come to you all at once, and it really comes to you in little bits and pieces?" she asked.

I nodded, instantly struck by the wisdom of her statement.

Her eyes lit up. "Well, I had one of those bits and pieces tonight."

"What happened?" I asked.

"When Isabelle's mom was driving us home, my favorite song came on the radio and we turned it up really loud and Isabelle and I started singing at the top of our lungs," she beamed.

"How fun," I laughed.

"Yeah," she nodded, laughing too. "I felt sooo happy."

"I'm glad," I told her, happy that she was happy. I kissed her goodnight, and left her room.

And, for a long time after that, I thought about what she said. Because she was right. Sometimes we expect happiness to come all at once . . . in a promotion, a relationship, a success, an achievement. But, really, happiness is all around us every day, in little bits and pieces.

In our favorite song coming on the radio, in an answered prayer, in a conversation with a friend, in the trees blooming in our yard, in our kids doing the dishwasher without being asked, in the sunshine coming through the bedroom window, in perfectly ripe tomatoes, or even in Katie's story about her own bits and pieces of happiness.

Bliss is like that too. We just need to train our eyes, and hearts, to see it. Sometimes as moms, as we go through our busy, hectic, fast-paced (and noisy!) days, we walk right past moments of bliss that are just waiting for us to take notice. Like the one morning in our house last year, when things got unusually quiet. I went upstairs to see why everything was so peaceful, half-expecting something to be wrong. Any mom knows that when things get silent, it usually means something's going on. But what I found was . . . blissful: Katie sitting in the sunshine reading, our cat Charlie curled up under her knees, and Luke relaxing a few feet away on the couch, our little dog Bailey on his lap.

After several weeks of sick kids (Katie had just gotten over strep throat, then pneumonia, and Luke had pneumonia too), it was a moment I was immediately thankful for. Both kids were feeling better, the house was calm, and everyone was content. Like the sun coming through the windows, the moment felt like a warm touch on my shoulder.

Bliss.

That day—that moment—I caught it. I recognized the moment for what it was, was overwhelmed with a feeling of gratefulness, and I literally stood there on the stairway, paused, soaking it in. It was the same way when Luke was about seven years old and sat on my lap. He had suddenly gotten independent at that age, not wanting me to hug him around his friends, call him "buddy," or kiss him when I dropped him off places. So it surprised me when, one morning as I was sitting at the kitchen table writing, he walked over and just sat on my lap. At first, I thought he was hurt or upset, because it seemed out of character for him at the time, so I asked him what was wrong.

I remember he turned and smiled, and said, "Nothing." Then he wrapped both his arms around my neck, rested his head on my shoulder, and hugged me.

I hugged him back. Tight. "Love you, Mom," he whispered.

"Love you, too," I said, wishing the moment would never end. But too quickly, it did, and after less than a minute, he hopped off my lap and ran upstairs to play.

And just like that, it was over.

Those pieces of bliss . . .

No matter how fast our kids grow, or how independent they become, bits and pieces like that never go away—they stay tucked away in our memories forever. But that's because we saw them for what they were. We stopped long enough to recognize them and appreciate them. We caught them when they happened. I often wonder, how many of these moments have I missed? How many times did I walk right past a moment like this because I was too hurried or rushed or stressed?

But when we open our eyes to the little bits and pieces of joy that are sprinkled throughout our days, we suddenly see them. We find them, as long as we're searching.

Be More Blissful: One of the best ways to capture the bliss moments is to write about them! Stop and think about a moment you want to capture, then take some time to write about it. You might even want to tuck it away to give to your kids when they are grown. I write Katie and Luke a letter each year about all that happened throughout the year that I wanted to capture, then I seal it and put it in a box. I plan to give them their boxes when they are older and move out.

Speaking of writing down the moments, to show you how it can help you capture the bliss, I thought I'd share a letter I wrote about Katie a few years ago at the end of summer:

August 16, 2010—This Beautiful End of Summer with My Little Girl

As I write this, Katie is playing Monopoly with a friend,

and Luke is in his room driving a remote control car around. I just finished doing some writing and was wrapping up a few things on my computer when I looked at my calendar and saw that I have a school check-in day with Katie at her new middle school this week.

Middle school.

I can hardly believe she's going into sixth grade, and as the date gets closer, I can't even think about it without getting choked up.

I'm not emotional about it because I'm sad.

I'm not sad.

I'm just . . . emotional.

It's the same way I felt when I walked her into preschool for the first time, her tiny hand holding tightly onto mine, her thumb in her mouth because she was a little unsure.

I felt like this her first day of kindergarten, too, as I hurried away after dropping her off, hiding my tears under my sunglasses, hoping nobody would notice I was crying.

It's not that I want her to stay young, and it's not that I don't want her to be away from home.

That's not it.

It's just that I'm amazed and overwhelmed and sentimental about the fact that she used to be a tiny baby in my arms, mostly sleeping or crying, and now she's on the brink of becoming a teenager, then a woman.

In seven years, I'll have raised a woman.

See? Here come the tears again.

'Mommy, we're going outside," she just called.

They must be done with Monopoly.

"Okay," I say, masking the emotion in my voice.

I remember when she was younger and I used to have to go outside with her.

I remember when I'd bring a blanket out on the grass and let her crawl around and play.

I remember the time when she was two and ate a flower and I called poison control in a panic.

And the time she was four and finger-painted hand-prints all over our white Labrador when I had gone inside to get the phone.

The memories . . .

they make me laugh and cry.

There are so many of them.

And I know there are more to come.

I know that.

It's not like her going into middle school means my journey as a mom is over.

Really, in so many ways, it's just beginning.

Maybe that's what my emotion is about . . . the changing season, the new phase.

Endings and beginnings.

It's just that I love her so much.

And with the school year starting in a week, and the fact that I know by now how fast the days, months, and years fly by,

I'm acutely aware of this time,

this moment,

this beautiful end of summer

with my little girl.

I love you, Katie.

—Mommy

Mom-to-Mom: Are you in a season of endings, or beginnings, or both? What about this time is hard for you, and what do you love the most about it? Search the pieces today, and capture those moments of bliss!

Heart-to-Heart: "There is a time for everything, and a season for every activity under the heavens."
—*Ecclesiastes 3:1 NIV*

Think about this past year for a moment. What seasons have you or your family been through? What has been the most difficult? The most joy-filled? If you could share one moment of bliss that stood out for you, what would that be?

A Mom's Prayer: *God, thank you for the seasons of my life, and my kids' lives. Thank you for the joy I've known, and thank you for all the moments I've had with my kids that will stay with me forever. Sometimes, I look forward to the future, when I think things will be better or easier. But I don't want to lose sight of all the blessings You've put in my life, today. Please open my eyes to look for the bliss in the bits and pieces of being a mom, every day. Amen.*

Tip #19

Love Being a Mom
(There's no other job like it!)

"Most folks are about as happy as they make up
their minds to be."
—Abraham Lincoln

When Luke was younger, he walked in the front door one day after school with a huge smile on his face and said proudly, "I wrote you a poem at school today."

"You did?" I smiled.

"Yeah. For Mother's Day. But I wanna read it to you now, okay?" He dropped his backpack on the floor and dug a piece of paper out of it. Then he plopped himself at the bottom of the stairs and looked up at me. "Ready?" he asked.

I almost told him I wanted to save the poem for Mother's Day, but I could tell how excited he was about what he wrote. So instead, I plopped down next to him. "Ready," I said.

He read it out loud:

"Mom, you feed me and hug me and love me all day.
When I do something wrong, you say it's okay.
You say it's okay almost every day.
That's how I know you love me today.
You're sweet and nice
and you taught me about Christ.

I can't ask for anything more,
so thank you for the stuff you've done before.
You treat me like a king.
And when my alarm goes ding
and I go downstairs
I don't have to guess, you're always there.
So I thank you for what you have done for me
from down in the dirt to high in the trees
and every day you remind me
that you love me."

Talk about bliss! I put my arm around him and squeezed his shoulder, tight. "I *love* that," I said, my voice catching.

His words touched something deep inside of me, and that day I was reminded of what it means to leave a legacy. I was reminded of the power of the little things we say and do. And I was reminded of the joy of being a mom.

I love the part in the movie *Prince Caspian*, where Lucy sees Aslan in the forest. "You've grown," she says to him.

"Every year you grow, so shall I," he says back.

And that's how it is with being a mom. With each year our kids grow, we grow too—as women, and as moms. It's a beautiful bond we have and it's a beautiful time in our lives, if only we can remember to see past the chaos and challenges.

With each trial and phase of motherhood, we learn and grow (or get stretched, pulled, contorted—you get it) as a person. With each joy and success, our hearts expand. And there's *so* much about that to love. Every minute we spend rocking our babies, changing diapers, kissing bruises, wiping tears, cleaning up the house, folding laundry, cooking dinners, volunteering at our kids' schools, driving around, watching practices and games, helping with homework, listening to heartbreak, encouraging, cheering, praying . . . loving . . . every minute counts.

Our job matters more than we can ever imagine. If you ever doubt that, mom, take a minute to think about these questions:

Be More Blissful: Ask Yourself . . .
1. Who is one person who has taught you an important lesson in life?
2. Who influenced you the most as a child?
3. Who has been there for you during both good and bad times?

As you answer those questions, think about why you chose the names you chose. Why did this person or these people have such a lasting influence on you? For me, it was the people who made me feel the most loved and who spent the most time with me that influenced me the most.

And that's what we do with our kids—take time and love them. The impact of that, and the effects on their lives, is far reaching. I got a huge reminder of this a few years ago. It was during baseball season, and Luke had just started experiencing a hitting slump. He began the season great, and then suddenly, game after game, he had a hard time hitting the ball. We explained that it happens to even the best players, but he was getting more and more discouraged.

One day, when Mike was outside practicing with him and I was upstairs in Katie's room, I heard Luke out the window. Frustrated, he said to Mike, "What's wrong with me, Dad?" It broke my heart.

The next morning before his game, he came and sat down on my bed. I could tell he was nervous about how he was going to do. "I have a feeling today's going to be your big day," I told him, trying to encourage him. "Just believe in yourself and pray. You can do it. You've done it before and you can do it again." He nodded, still unsure. So I said, "Just picture yourself outside playing with Dad and hitting the ball over the house like you do. Don't lose your confidence or doubt yourself. *Believe*, okay?"

It turns out the game that day was his best game ever. He hit three doubles and got the player of the game award. After the game, when he and I we were walking across the parking lot to the car, he looked up at me and said, "I remembered your advice, Mom."

I nonchalantly said, "To picture yourself hitting the ball over our house?"

"No." He shook his head and smiled. "To believe in myself. I didn't forget."

It choked me up. It was so humbling to think that

something I said helped him to believe in himself like that. That me—his mom—could impact him—his *heart*—like that.

> **Be More Blissful:** Reflect on a time you have impacted your kids positively. You have helped them more than you know, mom! Celebrate your successes and know how much you matter. Because you really, really do.

You may not feel important right now, mom, but you *are.* And you might not even be fully aware of the successes you've had as a mom. It can take years to see the fruit of our prayers and our efforts. But the next time you feel overwhelmed or that the rewards of parenting are missing, remember how much what you are doing matters. I was cleaning out Katie's room one weekend when I happened upon a poem she had written for me one year in school. It was titled, "What is a Mother?" and the first line read: *A mother is someone who takes care of people.*

At first, the sentence made me laugh. And I thought, *Yes.* A mother does take care of people. All the time!

But then my thoughts changed . . . and I was suddenly struck by the thought, *What is a mother?* And I paused and just soaked in the joy of being able to take care of and raise Katie and Luke. Our job as moms doesn't come with high pay or bonuses, stock options, or prime office space. But the rewards are so much greater. Look around you, mom; the rewards are everywhere.

Be More Blissful: Take some time right now to journal some of the rewards and special moments you've had as a mom. When we take time to remember the blessings, the bliss naturally comes with it.

Here are some of mine:

– Mike and I took the kids to Disneyland when they were about seven and nine. After we had gone on the Pirates of the Caribbean, as we walked back outside, Katie and Luke walked a few steps ahead of Mike and me. They talked excitedly to each other, both smiling and nodding their heads. Then they did something that totally surprised me; they reached for each other's hands. Mike nudged me and pointed at them. I nodded, choking back tears. They walked like that, hands swinging between them, the whole way to the next ride. I think it had been at least two years since I'd seen my kids holding hands with each other.

– One time when Katie was younger, she surprised me and changed the ring tone on my cell phone to be a recording of her own voice. Every time my phone rang, I got to hear her saying, "I love you, Mommy. I love you. You're the best mommy in the *whole* world. And I miss you right now. I love you, Mommy . . ." It was the best.

– Another time, I overheard Katie and Luke trying to decide what movie to watch.

"You can choose because it's your birthday tomorrow," he told her.

"I kind of want to watch a TV show and not a movie, but I don't want to hurt your feelings," she said back to him.

"That's okay," he answered. "You can do whatever you want. I don't mind. It's *your* birthday." Not the typical conversation when they are trying to agree on a show. I wish I could've bottled the moment and saved it forever.

– Oh, and then there was the time when I came home from being gone for a few hours and found two vases of flowers Katie and Luke had picked for me on the table.

When we take the time to remember moments like these and reflect on the rewards that come with being a mom, we bring joy to the surface. We brighten the bliss. And we appreciate the moments in front of us with a new sense of knowing that they are passing too quickly. I remember times when Katie and Luke were younger and things felt chaotic. I remember when I used to long for time to take a bath, or go for a walk, or even just a full hour by myself to write.

And just a few weeks ago, I found myself missing those days. I was sitting at a coffee shop, writing on my laptop, and right outside the window, there was a mom with a little boy on her lap . . .

He sipped his chocolate milk from a straw and leaned against her, the sunshine making his blond curls shine in the morning light. She ran her fingers through his hair, then tickled his back, making him laugh. He twisted to the side, and she kissed his forehead. Then, in a flash, he slid off her lap and ran around the patio, a constant motion, as most toddlers are.

An elderly man and his dog walked by, and the man stopped and smiled at the boy. He said something to the mom and she answered, smiling too. I thought he was probably asking her how old her son is, or maybe telling her how cute he is (because he was precious). The boy ran in circles and the man watched, his eyes almost misty. Maybe the man was recollecting when he was just a boy, or maybe he was thinking about his own children if he had any, or maybe he was contemplating the circle of life and how fast time flies.

Either way, I could relate. I've noticed lately that with Luke and Katie well past the toddler stage, whenever I see babies or little ones like this, I can't help but remember how precious those times were.

Just as I was thinking this, the mom turned and looked at me through the window. We smiled at each other. Maybe she was thinking how nice it would be to have time alone at a coffee shop like I have—just me and my big cup of coffee and my laptop. Maybe she was longing for the day she'd have a couple of hours to herself too.

And yet there I was looking at her on the other side of the glass, missing the moments she was experiencing right then.

As her son crawled back up on her lap, I wanted to go outside and sit down next to her and say *enjoy it. Enjoy every second, because even if it doesn't always feel like it, this time is magical.*

I wanted to tell her that what everyone says is true: *it really does go faster than you think. And on the days when your son is crying and you feel like all you do is hold him and carry him around and clean up after him . . .*

hold him closer,

and kiss his little forehead more,

and savor the smell of his sunshine hair and the sound of his voice and the feel of his tiny hands

in yours.

Because sooner than you know it,

he'll be twelve or fourteen,

and he'll be too big to crawl up on your lap

or snuggle against you while he drinks chocolate milk

in the morning light

on the patio of a coffee shop.

Sometimes we need reminders like this to help us appreciate the moments right in front of us. Because those moments are precious and fleeting, and before long, they will be gone, too.

> **Be More Blissful:** In every moment today, take this verse to heart (say it out loud if needed!): "Be joyful always."—*1 Thessalonians 5:16 GNT*

Sometimes, we need to make the decision to be joyful, and our feelings will follow.

The moments pass quickly. The days whiz by. Yet you are a constant for your kids, mom. And you can be the bearer of bliss.

Mom-to-Mom: What do you love most about motherhood? What brings you the most joy? What are you most thankful for?

Heart-to-Heart: "Therefore my brothers and sisters, stand firm. Let nothing move you. Always give yourselves fully to the work of the Lord, because you know that your labor in the Lord is not in vain."
—*1 Corinthians 15:58 NIV*

Do you sometimes wonder if you are making a difference? When do you feel that way, and why? Even though it can be easy to feel that way, I promise you, your labor is not in vain, moms!

A Mom's Prayer: *God, thank you that my work as a mom is not in vain. Even on the days I feel invisible or unappreciated, You see all I do. Please help me to stand firm for my family. Give me strength, wisdom, patience, and, most* *of all, joy. Help me to focus on the smiles and the laughter, not on the challenges and worries. Help me to create a home where happiness grows and flourishes. I will hold on to Your promises as I parent. Thank you for my kids and the honor of being their mom. Amen.*

Tip #20

Don't Go It Alone
(You have God on your team!)

"For I can do everything through Christ,
who gives me strength."
—*Philippians 4:14 NLT*

We try to say prayers as a family every night. Even as the kids have gotten older, it's part of our bedtime routine and I love the time together—the craziness of the day settled, for the moment. I love hearing the things Katie and Luke pray for and the way it gives me a glimpse of what's on their minds.

One night, after the kids had gone to bed, Katie came back downstairs to get a glass of water. After she filled her glass, she walked over to me and gave me a hug. She held on for a little while. And before she let go, she whispered, "Dear Lord, Thank you for Mommy and Daddy and my brother."

It was one of those moments where you're caught off-guard in the sweetest way. It was neat to see something we do regularly with our kids become something Katie did on her own. She's seen me praying, we've prayed together, and now she was praying on her own. Her youth pastor talked about this in a parent meeting not too long ago. He gave an analogy that I loved, saying that raising a child is a lot like teaching them to ride a bike. For a while you run behind them, pushing them and holding on tight. And at some point, you start to let go.

Slowly.

Tentatively.

You might even run beside them, your hands on the handlebars or the back of the seat, just in case, hoping they'll remember what you've taught them about balance, and putting on the breaks, and watching where they're going. And then . . . you realize they are pedaling on their own. Sure, they'll fall every now and then. And you'll need to be there to dust them off, and maybe kiss a scraped elbow or two. But it's an awesome feeling to see them ride.

And that's how God feels about us, moms.

Sure, we wobble sometimes in this parenting journey. Sometimes, we even fall flat on our face. But, just like we do with our kids when they stumble, He helps us back up. He steadies us as we start to ride again, and he smiles as our pedals quicken. And the only difference is He never lets go.

Whatever you are facing as a mom right now, God is rooting for you. Pray about what you are going through. Even if the thing you are struggling with is small, or you feel like it's something you should have figured out on your own, don't feel like it isn't important enough for God, or that He wouldn't be able to help.

A few summers ago, Katie and I pulled up to the pool where she practices for swim team every day. She opened the car door to get out. "I hope the snow cone truck is here after practice," she said. (A local snow cone company had been parking their truck near the pool most days.)

"I hope so too," I told her.

"Pray for it to be here, okay Mommy?" She smiled and got out of the car.

"I will," I said as she started to close the door.

But, then, instead of walking away, she suddenly hopped back in the front seat, bowed her head, and folded her hands. "Pray *now*," she said. And so we did. Right there in the parking lot, with the car running, my teenage daughter and I prayed for that snow cone truck to come after practice. When we were done, she got out of the car and ran off to the pool. And I drove away with a huge smile on my face.

I loved the way she wanted to pray *right then*. I loved her childlike faith and the way she wanted to take even a small desire like a snow cone to the throne of the Maker of the Universe. I loved her acceptance and *expectation* of God's involvement in every detail of her life.

We moms should be like that too. We don't need to wait on praying, or only pray for the "big" things. God cares about every detail of our lives, and that includes our parenting, our crazy days, our exhaustion, or whatever we are going through. It includes our kids and what they are going through too.

When you have a challenge with your child, do you worry about it or do you pray? Do you talk to your husband about it, or instantly try to correct the behavior . . . or do you pray? God doesn't want us to hold back from talking to Him just because we think our requests aren't important enough, or because we might feel self-ish for asking, or because we forget that He cares about everything.

He is God, yes . . . yet He's our Friend and Counselor who cares about even the tiniest details of our lives. Even when we don't know Him, He knows us. He knows the number of hairs on our head. He collects our tears in a bottle. And He wants to be involved in every aspect of our lives, big *and* small. Nothing is too insignificant for Him. *He cares.* And he doesn't want us to wait to ask Him either. Like Katie did that day in the car, He wants us to involve Him *now*. To seek him now. To pray now. Even if it that prayer *is* for something like a snow cone.

Oh, and in case you're wondering, the truck wasn't there after practice that day. But even though Katie was momentarily disappointed, I loved how she responded . . . "Well let's pray really hard tonight for it to be there tomorrow, okay?" So that night we did. And the next day, it was.

God cares about your parenting struggles and challenges, both big and small. And He has great plans for you *and* your kids. I love the reminder of that in this verse:

> "For I know the plans I have for you,
> says the Lord,
> plans to prosper you and not harm you,
> plans to give you a hope and a future.
> Then you will call on me and come and
> pray to me,

and I will listen to you.
You will seek me and find me
when you seek me with all your heart."
—*Jeremiah 29:11-13*

And I love the reminder that we have to call on Him, to come to Him and pray to Him. When we do that and seek Him with all our heart, we will find Him.

> **Be More Blissful: Have you forgotten that God has good plans for you and your kids? Have you been trying to do it all on your own? Is there something you could use help with right now, but have forgotten to pray about? Stop, pray, and seek Him with your whole heart. Find peace and strength in Him; He will hear you.**

Though the journey of motherhood is different for all of us, it doesn't have to be about "winging it" for any of us. God is on our team, waiting to help. When we remember that, and when we shift our perspective to see—truly see—the moments of joy that are all around us in this parenting journey, somehow all of the stressful or not-so-glamorous moments that come with being a mom don't seem so bad.

And that will help us—*and* our kids—to feel absolutely, positively blissful.

Be More Blissful: Did you know the Bible is full of answers to your parenting challenges? If you've never read the Bible before, try starting with the book of Psalms, a beautiful book filled with hope and every kind of emotion you can think of. It's great to see that we can be real with God about all the things we face as moms.

Mom-to-Mom: What is one area you might need to rely on God more in your parenting or your family? Have you opened up your heart to Him yet?

Heart-to-Heart: "For I know the plans I have for you, says the Lord, plans to prosper you and not harm you, plans to give you a hope and a future. Then you will call on me and come and pray to me, and I will listen to you. You will seek me and find me when you seek me with all your heart."
—*Jeremiah 29:11-13 NIV*

When we seek God, He promises we will find Him. Don't do parenting alone. God has amazing plans for you and your family, mom. Lean on Him and call on Him. He will listen to you, build you up, give you exactly what you need, and sustain you, even in the tough times.

A Mom's Prayer: *Dear God, I am so thankful to be a mom. Thank you for giving me my children. Thank you for the plans you have for me and my family. Help me to raise them to love You and to love others. Help me to remember that You are by my side, every minute of this journey. Please fill me with Your joy, and please help me to embrace every single moment of bliss. Amen.*

Finding Mommy Bliss is now on Snippet

To download the exciting, multimedia companion piece to this book—complete with video and audio of Genny, as well as photos behind the stories she shares—download her Snippet, packed with extras:

www.thesnippetapp.com/gennyheikka

Finding Mommy Bliss is also available in traditional eBook format on Kindle and Amazon.

ABOUT THE AUTHOR

Genny Heikka is an author, speaker, and passionate mentor to moms and writers. From mentoring teen moms through Youth for Christ and serving as Mentor Mom Coordinator for MOPS, to sharing about writing and publishing on her podcast, Genny has a passion for encouraging others. Before having kids, she was a manager at a global computer company and was busy climbing the corporate ladder. But after quitting her job to be a stay-at-home mom, she rediscovered her love of writing and set out to pursue her dream of becoming an author.

Today, she lives in Northern California with her husband and two kids, where she balances writing with motherhood and loves both. She's written seven children's books and regularly contributes to a variety of magazines and websites. Her work has been published in *Kirtsy Takes a Bow: A Celebration of Women's Favorites Online*, as well as two mentoring resources by TheMomInitiative.com: *Facing our Fears – 31 Stories from M.O.M.* and *Overwhelmed – 31 Stories from M.O.M.* She also reviews books for the *San Francisco Book Review* and the *Sacramento Book Review*, and co-hosts The Part Time Author podcast in iTunes.

Connect with Genny:
Website – gennyheikka.com
Facebook – facebook.com/GennyHeikkaAuthor
Twitter – twitter.com/GennyHeikka